Fun and Easy! Korean Picture Dictionary

marketing@newampersand.com

Ordering Information: Quantity sales. Special discounts are available on quantity purchases by corporations, associations, and others. For details, contact the publisher at the email address above.

Printed in the United States of America

ISBN-13: 979-1188195060

Table of Contents

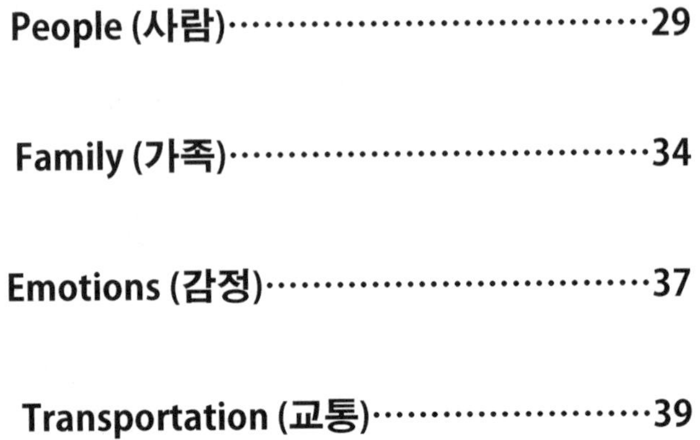

Table of Contents

BODY(신체)

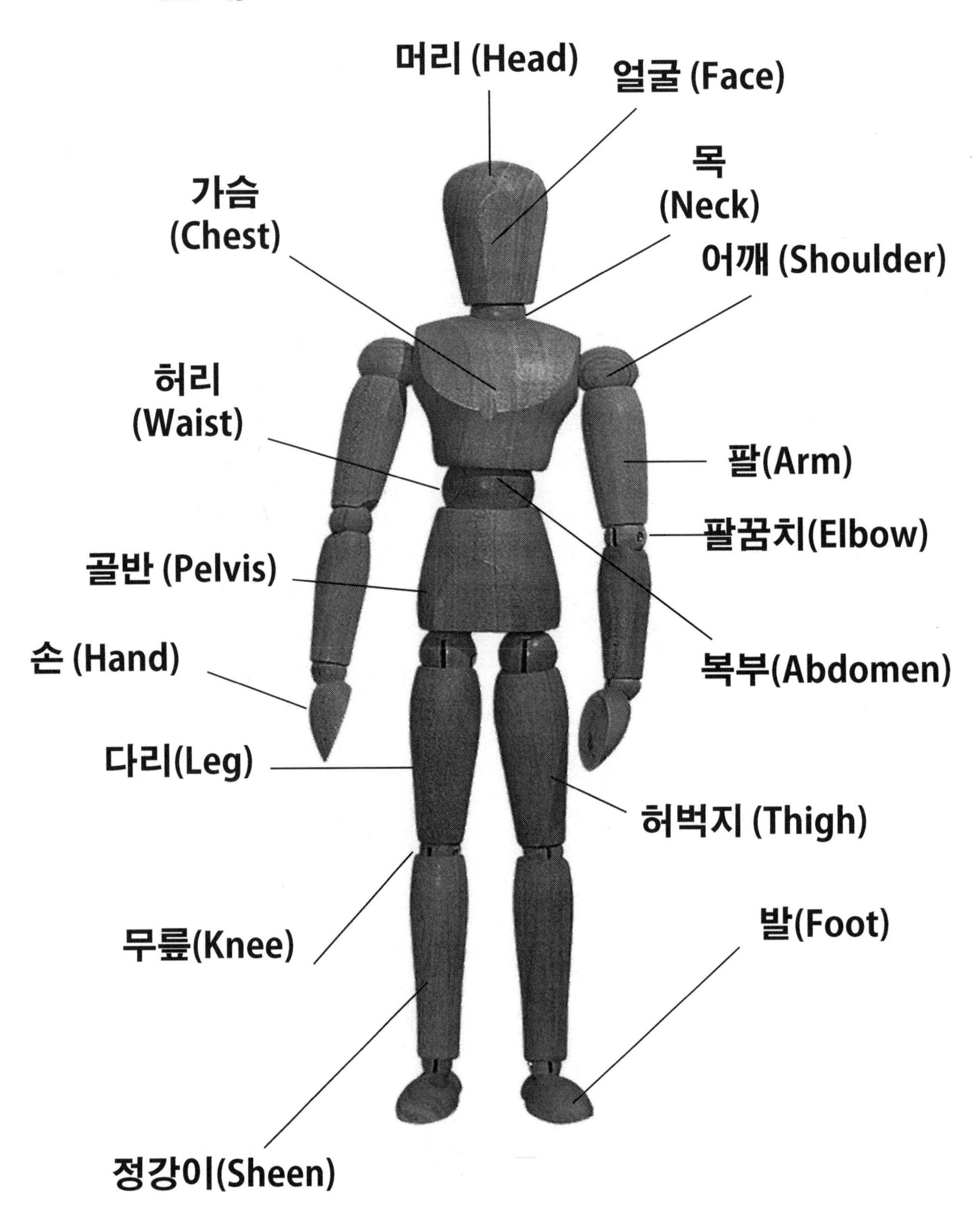
머리 (Head)
얼굴 (Face)
목
(Neck)
가슴
(Chest)
어깨 (Shoulder)
허리
(Waist)
팔(Arm)
팔꿈치(Elbow)
골반 (Pelvis)
손 (Hand)
복부(Abdomen)
다리(Leg)
허벅지 (Thigh)
발(Foot)
무릎(Knee)
정강이(Sheen)

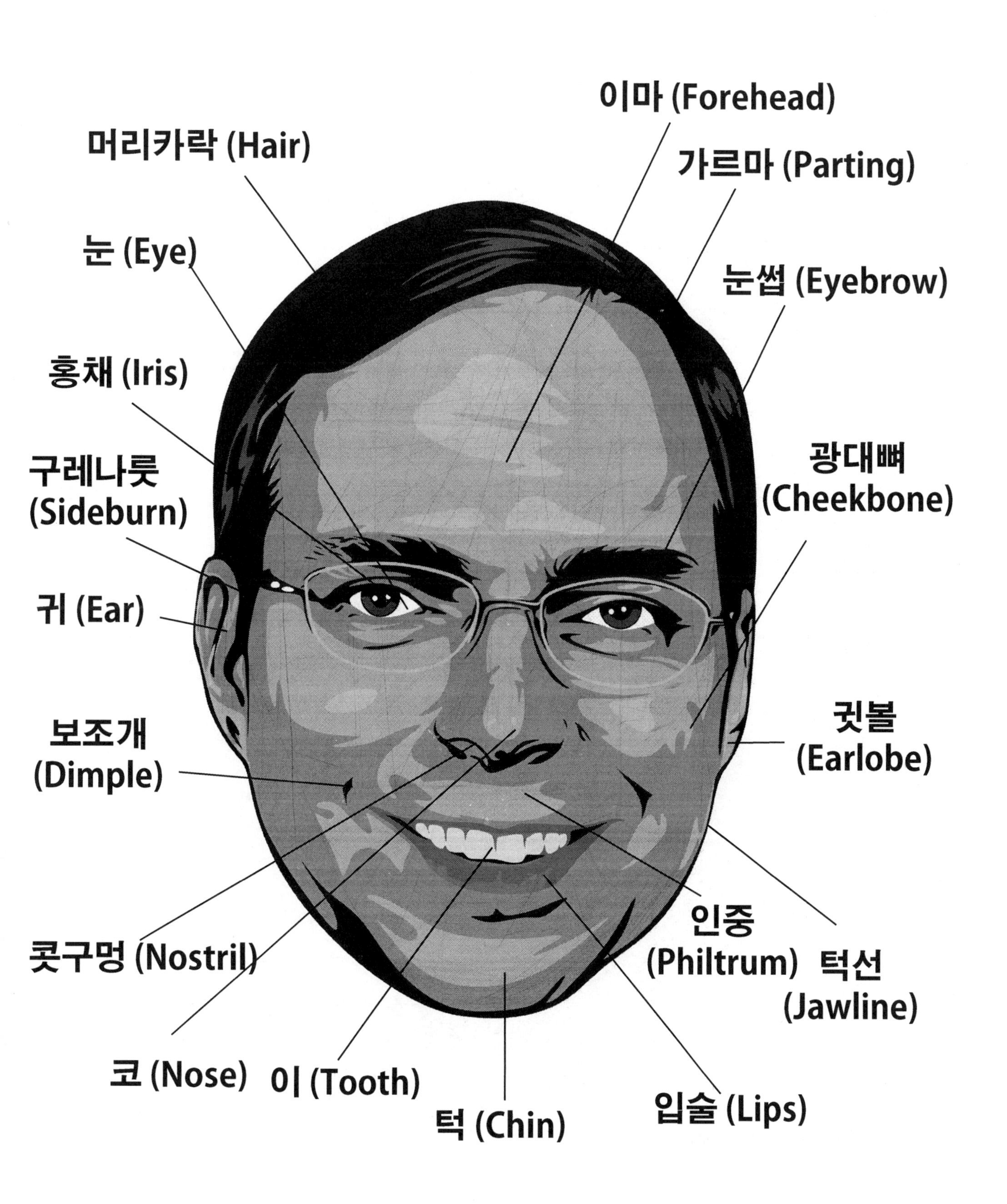
이마 (Forehead)
머리카락 (Hair)
가르마 (Parting)
눈 (Eye)
눈썹 (Eyebrow)
홍채 (Iris)
광대뼈
(Cheekbone)
구레나룻
(Sideburn)
귀 (Ear)
귓볼
(Earlobe)
보조개
(Dimple)
인중
(Philtrum)
턱선
(Jawline)
콧구멍 (Nostril)
코 (Nose)
이 (Tooth)
턱 (Chin)
입술 (Lips)

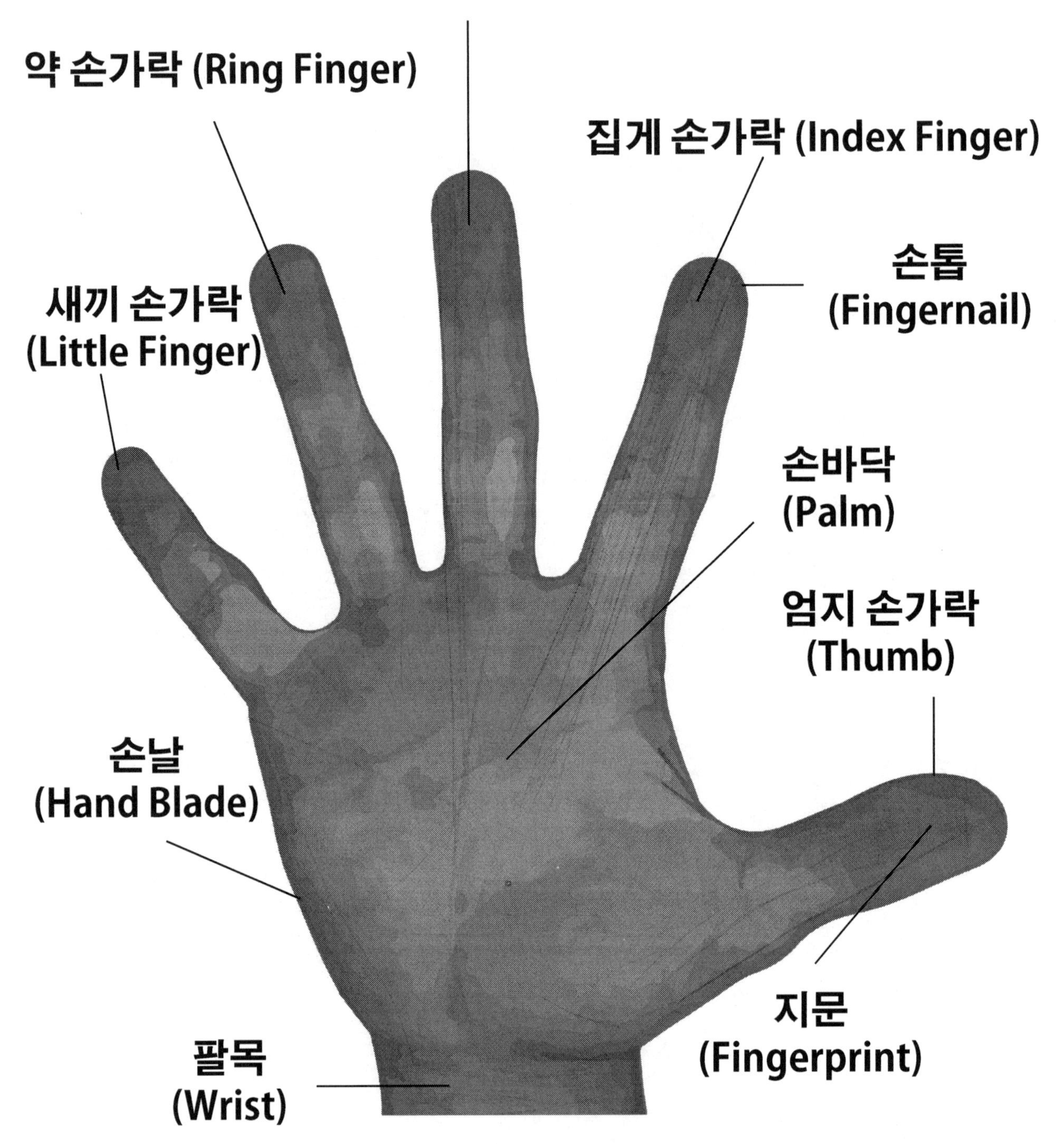
가운뎃 손가락 (Middle Finger)
약 손가락 (Ring Finger)
집게 손가락 (Index Finger)
손톱
(Fingernail)
새끼 손가락
(Little Finger)
손바닥
(Palm)
엄지 손가락
(Thumb)
손날
(Hand Blade)
지문
(Fingerprint)
팔목
(Wrist)

가운뎃 손가락 (Middle Finger)

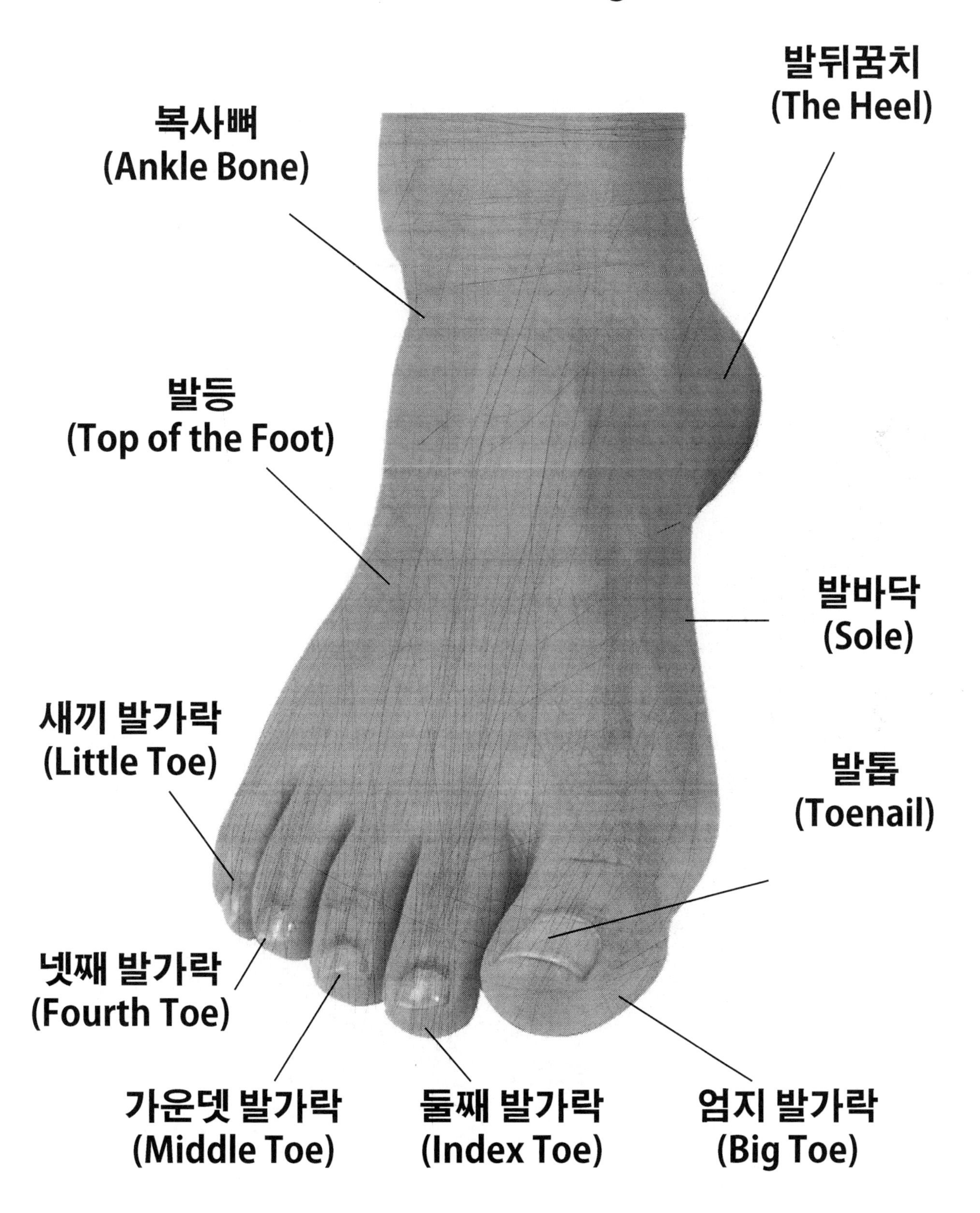

EXPRESSIONS(표현)

머리가 아파요.
My head hurts.

발톱을 깎았어요.
I cut my toenails.

발뒤꿈치가 까졌어요.
I skinned the back of my feet.

제 이상형은 눈썹이 짙은 남자입니다.
My ideal man is a man with thick eyebrows.

용의자는 지문을 남겼습니다.
The suspect left a fingerprint.

팔목을 잡다.
Grab somebody by the wrist.

콧구멍을 벌름거리다.
Flare one`s nostrils.

가르마를 타다.
Part one`s hair.

이마가 벗겨진
Bald at the forehead.

발바닥에 물집이 생겼어요.
I`ve got blisters on the soles of my feet.

HOME(집)

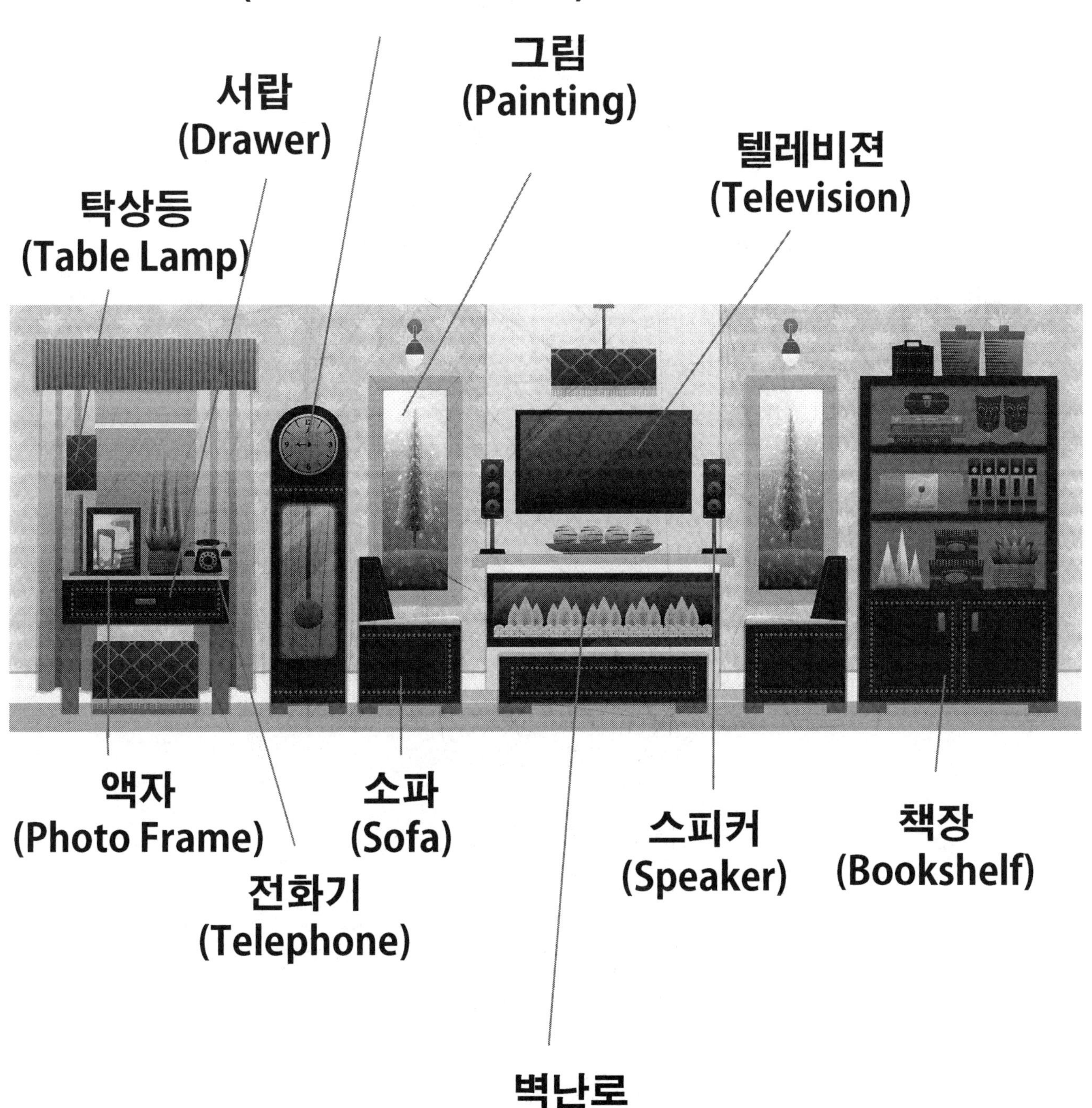

괘종시계
(Grandfather Clock)
그림
(Painting)
서랍
(Drawer)
텔레비젼
(Television)
탁상등
(Table Lamp)
액자
(Photo Frame)
소파
(Sofa)
전화기
(Telephone)
스피커
(Speaker)
책장
(Bookshelf)
벽난로
(Fireplace)

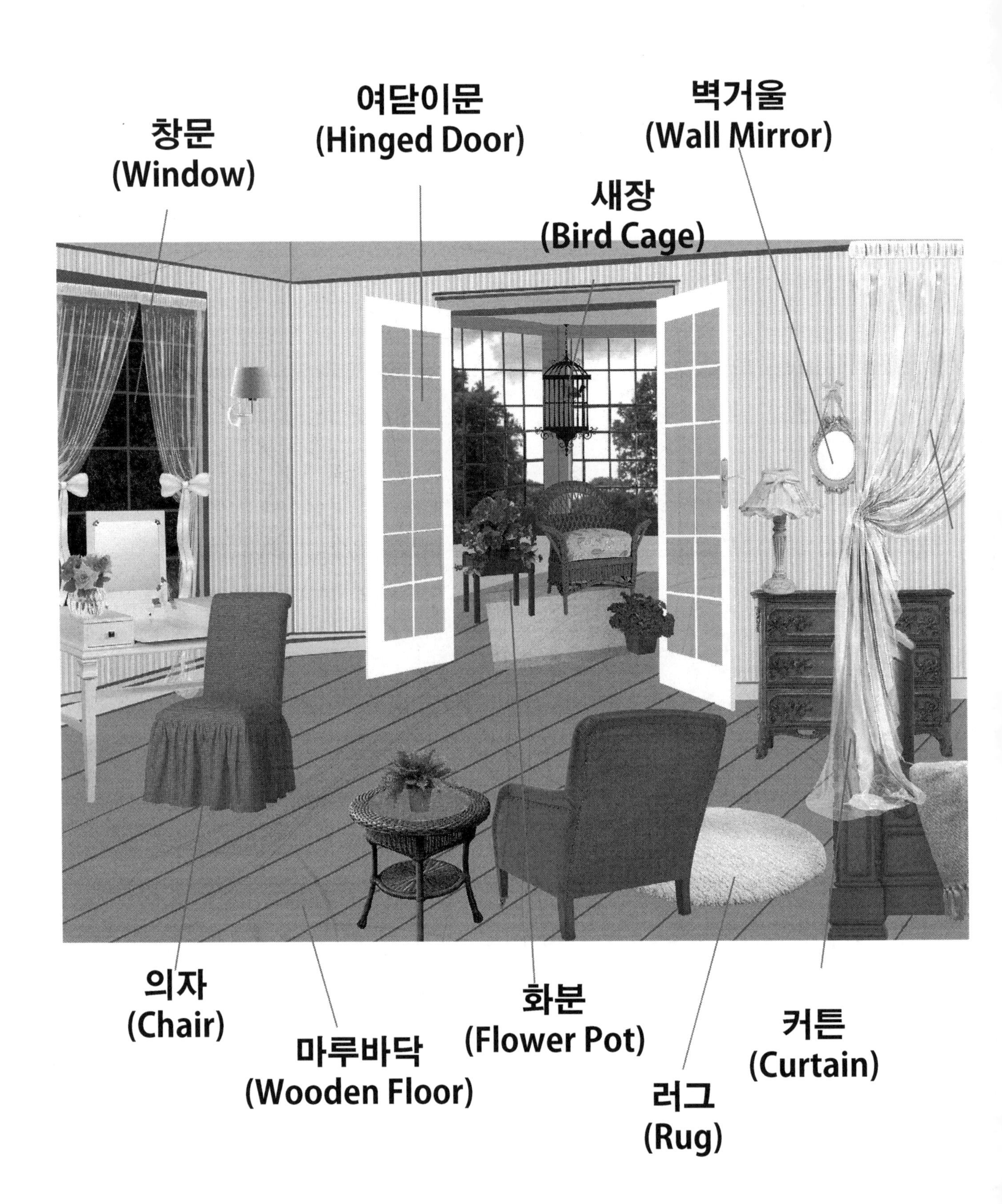
창문
(Window)
여닫이문
(Hinged Door)
벽거울
(Wall Mirror)
새장
(Bird Cage)
의자
(Chair)
마루바닥
(Wooden Floor)
화분
(Flower Pot)
러그
(Rug)
커튼
(Curtain)

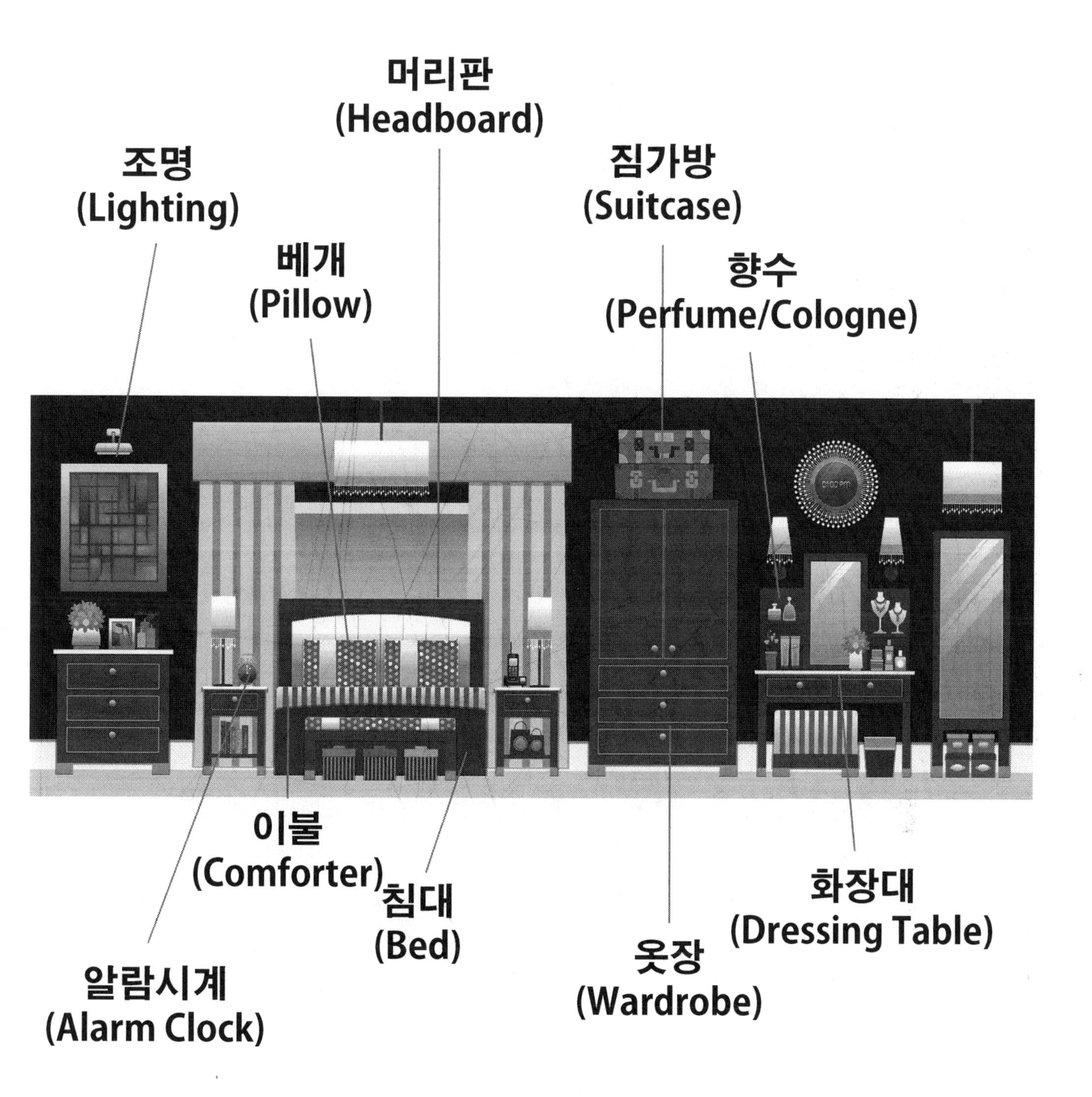
머리판
(Headboard)
조명
(Lighting)
짐가방
(Suitcase)
베개
(Pillow)
향수
(Perfume/Cologne)
이불
(Comforter)
침대
(Bed)
화장대
(Dressing Table)
옷장
(Wardrobe)
알람시계
(Alarm Clock)

세면대
(Basin)
목욕가운
(Bathrobe)
샤워실
(Shower Stall)
타월/수건
(Towel)
칫솔/치약
(Toothbrush/Toothpaste)
체중계
(Scale)
비누/샴푸/바디워시
(Soap/Shampoo/
Body Wash)
욕조
(Bathtub)
휴지
(Toilet Paper)
면도기
(Razor/Shaver)

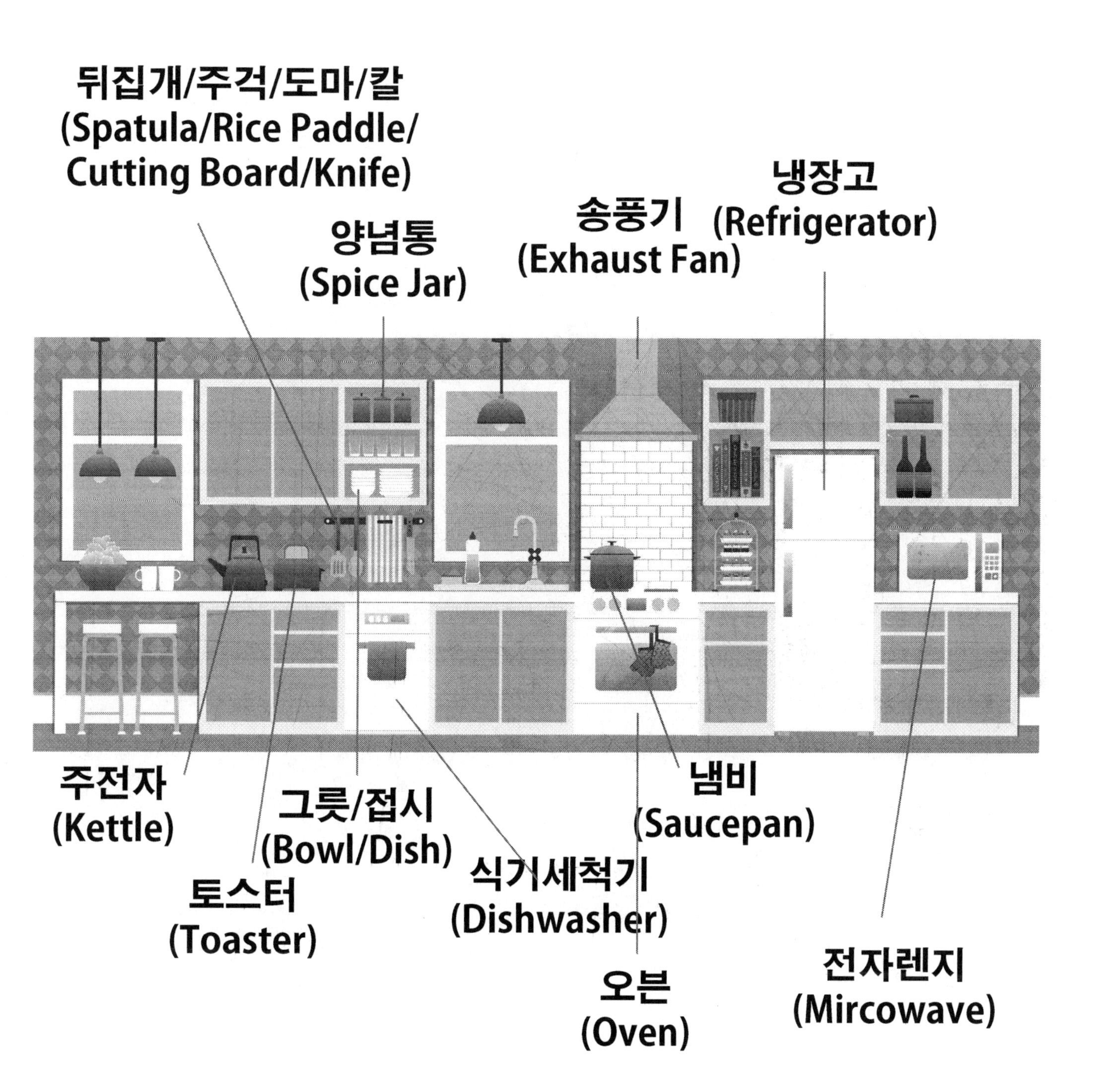

뒤집개/주걱/도마/칼
(Spatula/Rice Paddle/
Cutting Board/Knife)
양념통
(Spice Jar)
송풍기
(Exhaust Fan)
냉장고
(Refrigerator)
주전자
(Kettle)
그릇/접시
(Bowl/Dish)
토스터
(Toaster)
식기세척기
(Dishwasher)
냄비
(Saucepan)
오븐
(Oven)
전자렌지
(Mircowave)

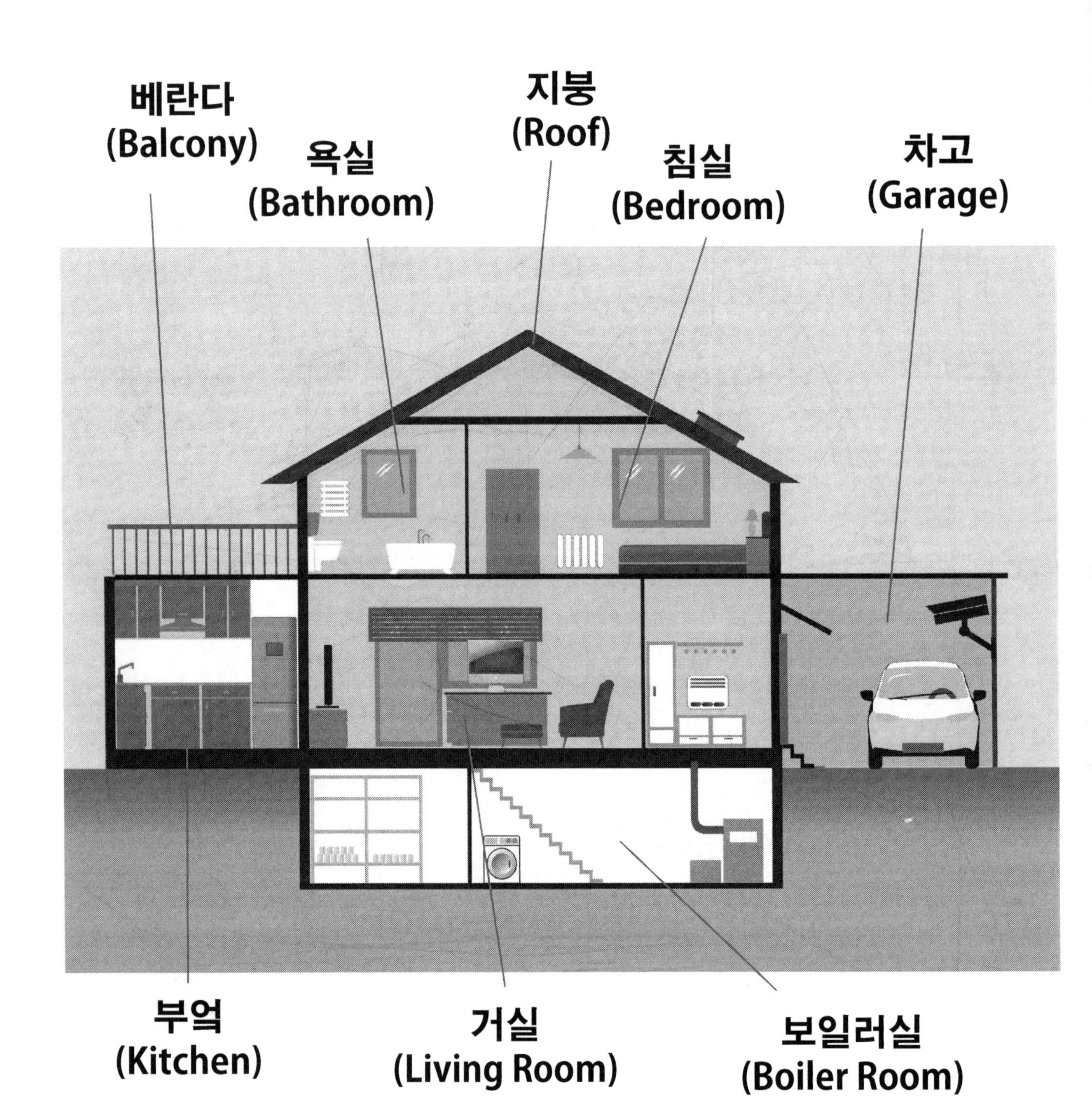
베란다
(Balcony)
욕실
(Bathroom)
지붕
(Roof)
침실
(Bedroom)
차고
(Garage)
부엌
(Kitchen)
거실
(Living Room)
보일러실
(Boiler Room)

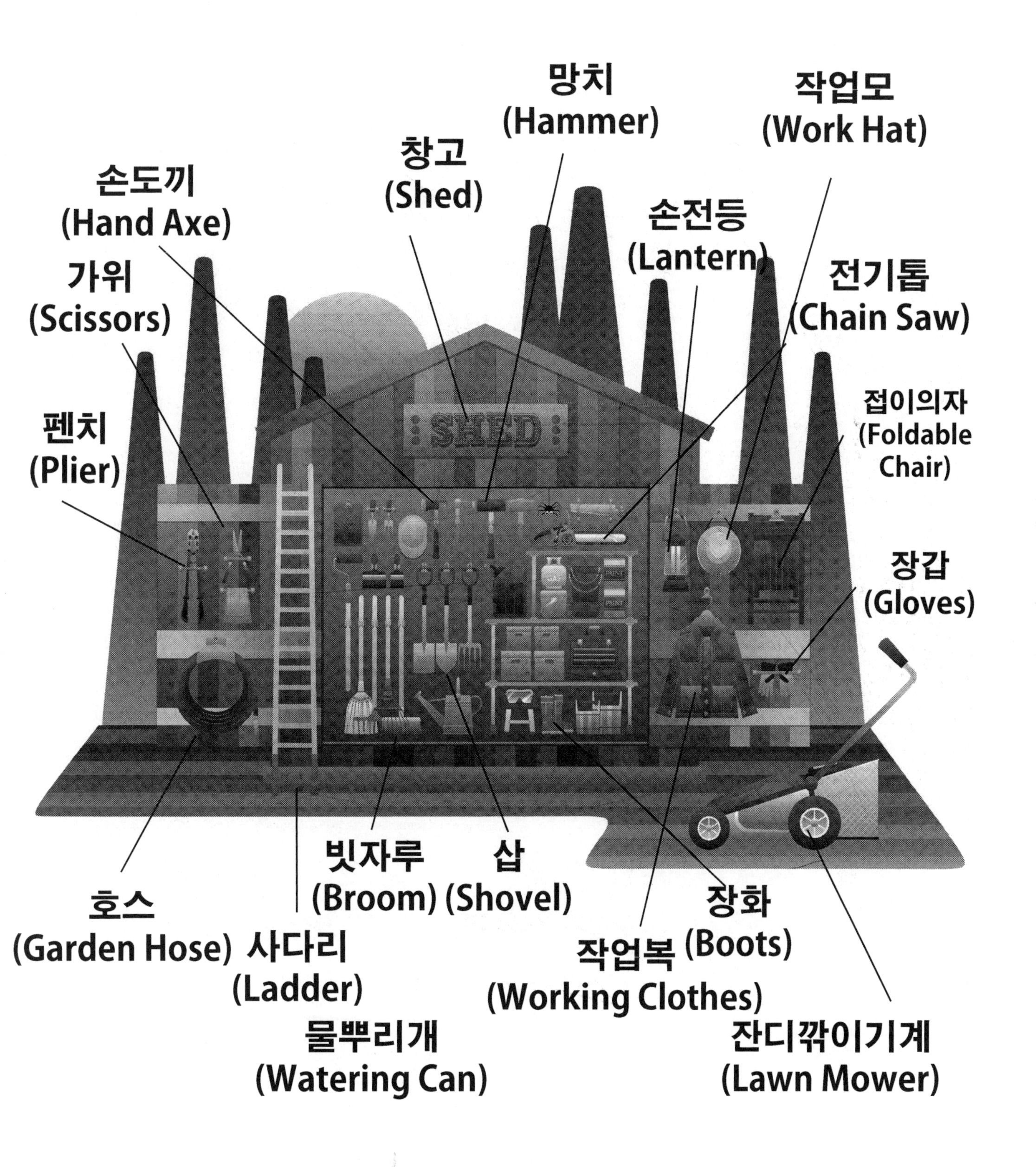
망치
(Hammer)
작업모
(Work Hat)
창고
(Shed)
손도끼
(Hand Axe)
손전등
(Lantern)
가위
(Scissors)
전기톱
(Chain Saw)
SHED
접이의자
(Foldable
Chair)
펜치
(Plier)
장갑
(Gloves)
빗자루
(Broom)
삽
(Shovel)
호스
(Garden Hose)
사다리
(Ladder)
장화
(Boots)
작업복
(Working Clothes)
물뿌리개
(Watering Can)
잔디깎이기계
(Lawn Mower)

EXPRESSIONS(표현)

소파에 앉아서 TV를 보고있어요.
I am watching TV sitting on a sofa .

벽에 액자를 걸다.
Hang a framed picture on the wall.

벽난로에서 장작이 타고 있다.
Wood is burning in the fireplace.

의자에 앉다.
Sit on a chair.

창문을 열어라 (command).
Open the window.

서랍을 닫아라 (command).
Close the drawer.

탁상등을 꺼라 (command).
Turn off the table lamp.

화분에 물을 주다.
Water the flower pot.

책장에 책이 하나도 없다.
There are no books on the bookshelf.

스피커가 너무 시끄럽다.
The speaker is too loud.

HOUSEHOLD ITEMS (생활용품)

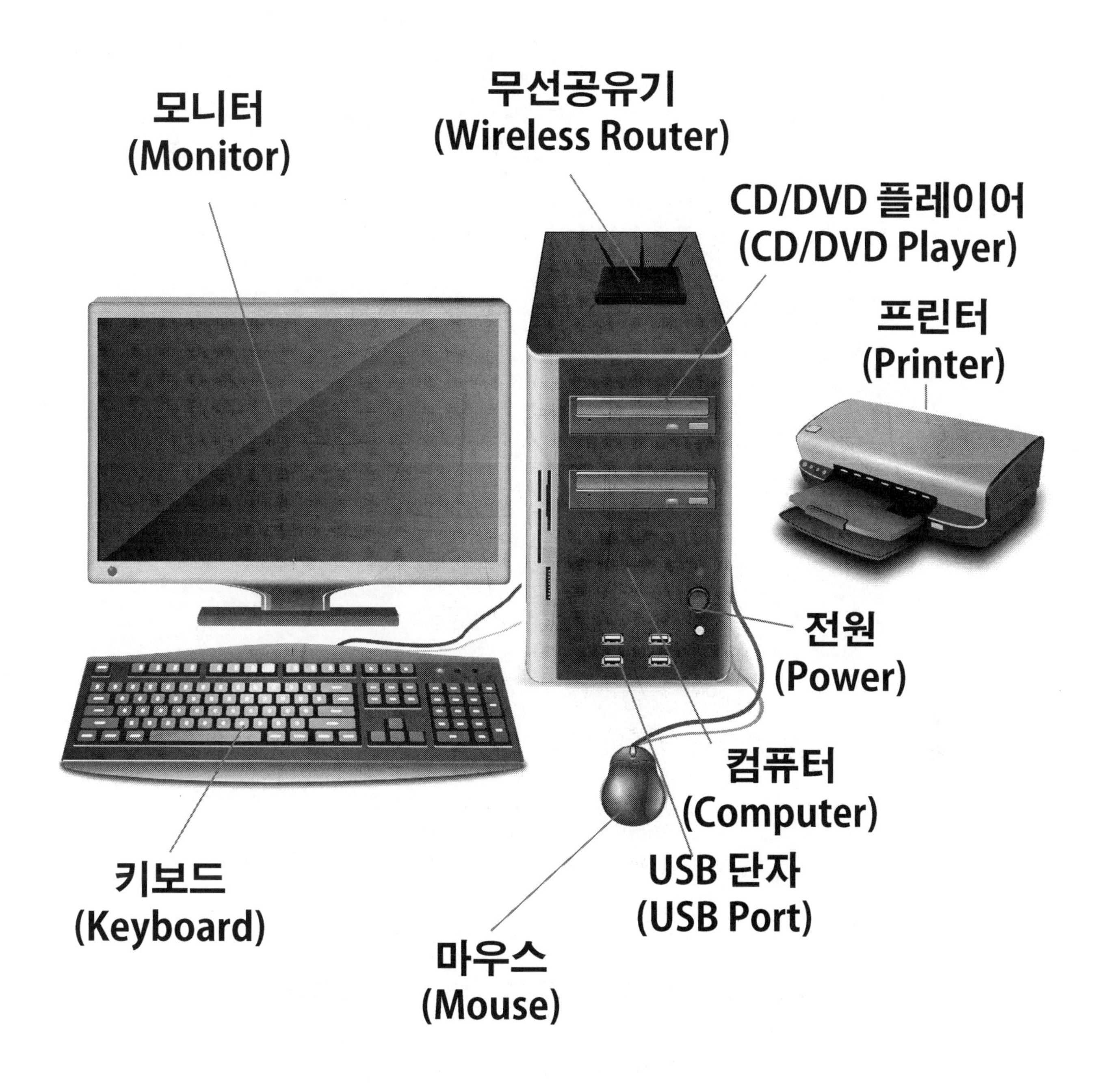

핸드폰 (Cell Phone)

라디오 (Radio)

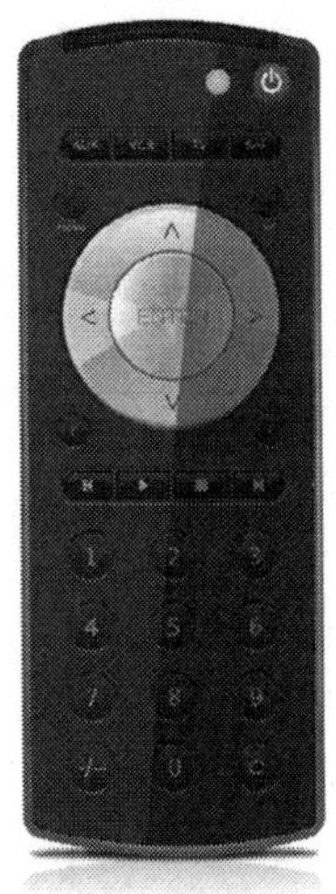

리모콘
(Remote Control)

지갑 (Wallet)

빨래판 (Washboard)

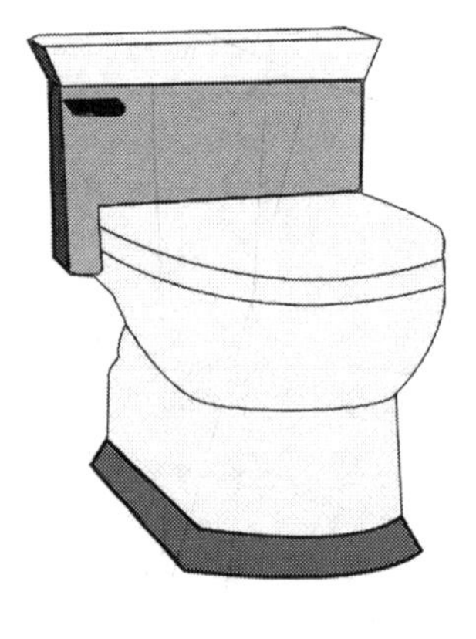

변기 (Toilet)

EXPRESSIONS(표현)

핸드폰이없으면 불안하다.
I feel anxious without my cell phone.

지갑을 잃어버렸다.
I lost my wallet.

변기가 막혔다.
The toilet got clogged.

이불과 베게 잊지마!
Don`t forget the pillow and comforter.

컴퓨터 껐어?
Did you turn off the computer?

창고에가서 전기톱 가져와!
Go to the shed and bring the chainsaw.

오븐에서 타는 냄새가 난다.
It smells like burning in the oven.

냉장고에 우유가 있나?
Do we have milk in the fridge?

그릇을 깨뜨렸어 !
I broke a dish!

알람시계 맞춰놨어?
Did you set the alarm clock?

20

SUPERMARKET(슈퍼마켓)

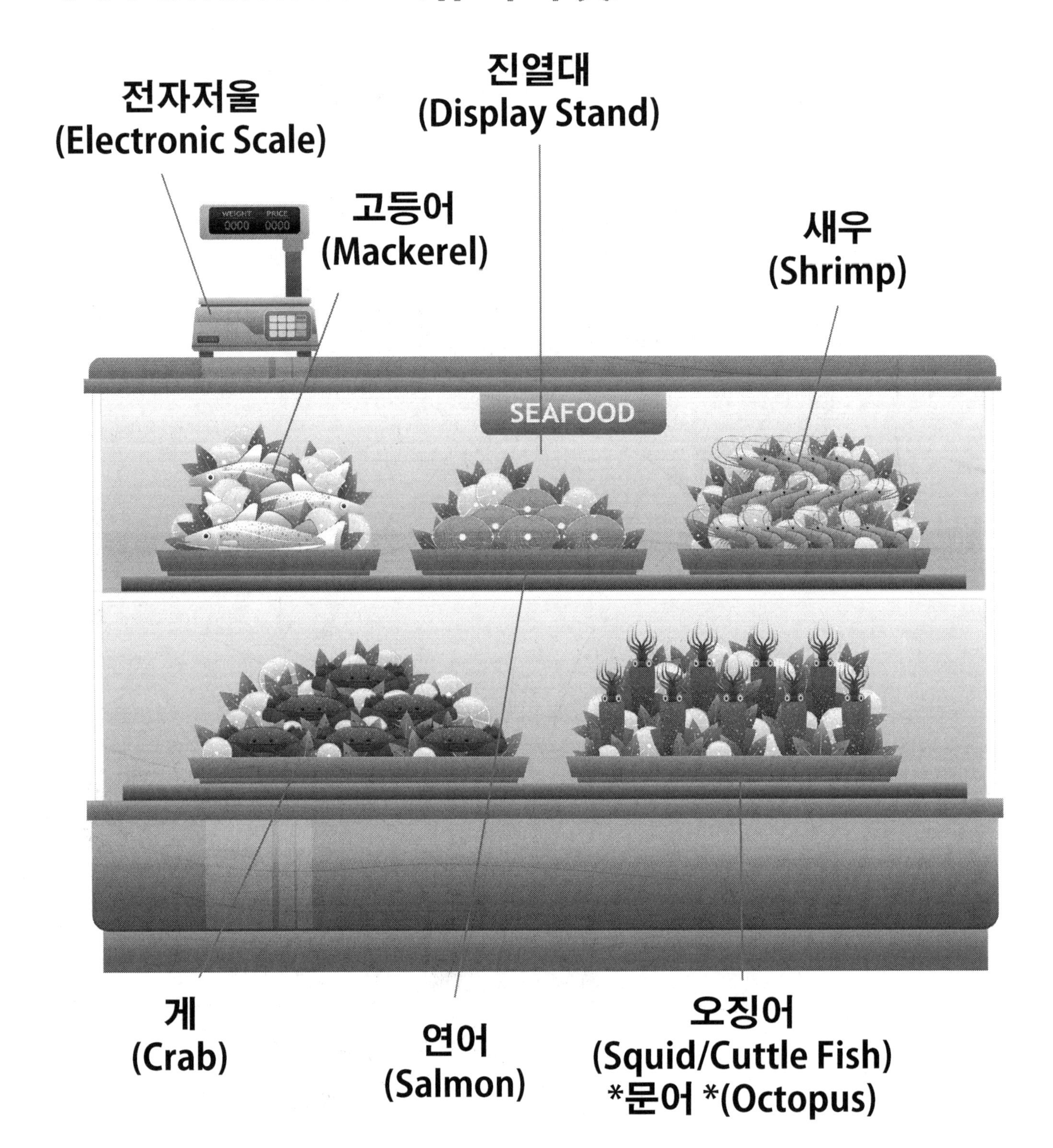

샴푸/컨디셔너
(Shampoo/Conditioner)
샤워젤
(Shower Gel)
SHAMPOO
CONDITIONER
SHAMPOO
CONDITIONER
SHOWER GEL
SHOWER GEL
SHOWER GEL
SHOWER GEL
치약
(Toothpaste)
비누
(Soap)
SOAP
FACEWASH
HANDWASH
TOOTHPASTE
마루 세척제
(Floor Cleaner)
주방용 세제
(Dish Soap)
DISHWASH
FLOOR CLEANER
ALL PURPOSE CLEANER
다용도 세척제
(All-Purpose
Cleaner)
LAUNDRY
BLEACH
세탁용 세제
(Laundry Detergent)
표백제
(Bleach)

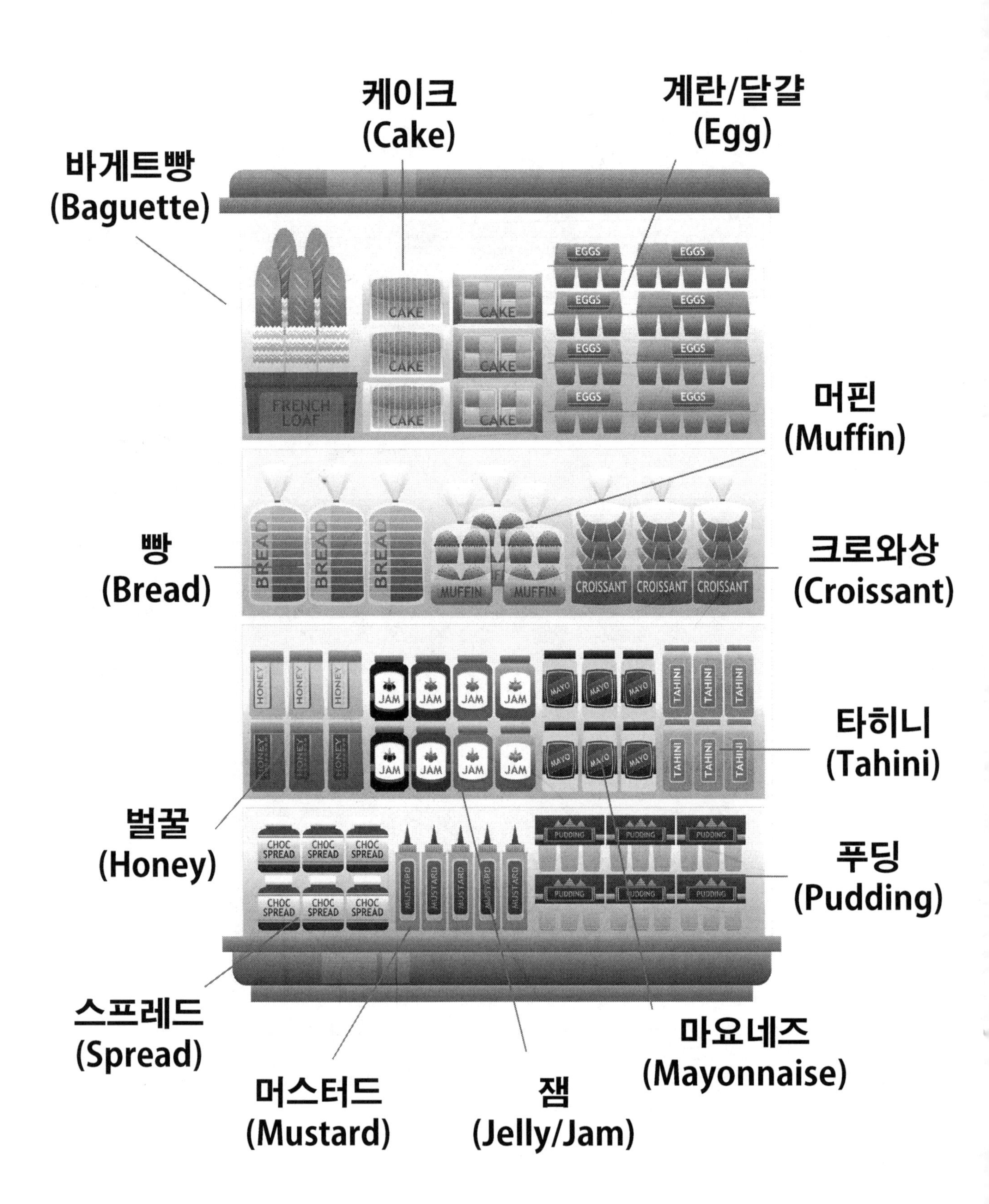
케이크
(Cake)
계란/달걀
(Egg)
바게트빵
(Baguette)
EGGS
CAKE
FRENCH LOAF
머핀
(Muffin)
빵
(Bread)
BREAD
MUFFIN
CROISSANT
크로와상
(Croissant)
HONEY
JAM
MAYO
TAHINI
타히니
(Tahini)
벌꿀
(Honey)
CHOC SPREAD
MUSTARD
PUDDING
푸딩
(Pudding)
스프레드
(Spread)
마요네즈
(Mayonnaise)
머스터드
(Mustard)
잼
(Jelly/Jam)

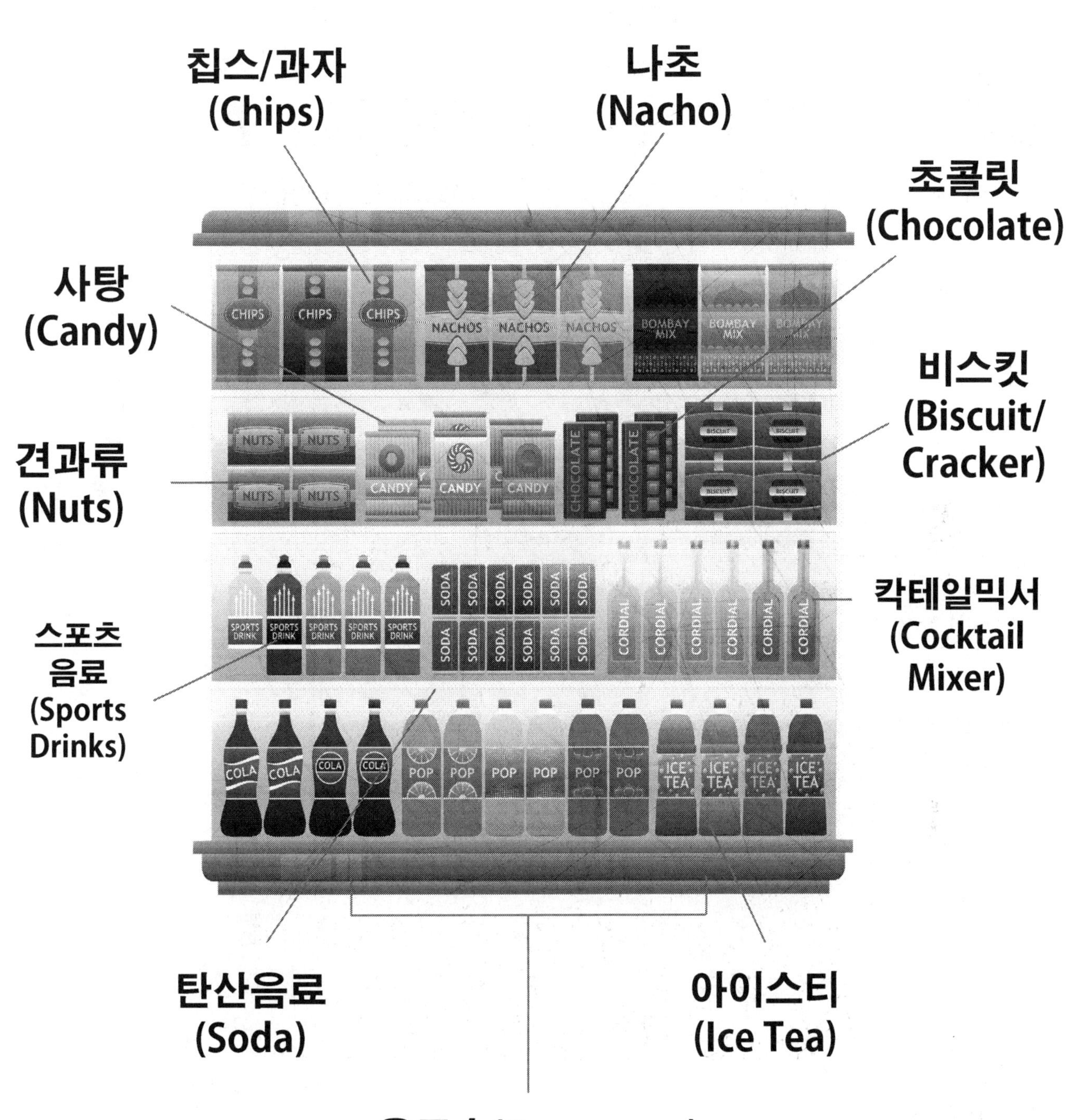
칩스/과자
(Chips)
나초
(Nacho)
초콜릿
(Chocolate)
사탕
(Candy)
비스킷
(Biscuit/
Cracker)
견과류
(Nuts)
칵테일믹서
(Cocktail
Mixer)
스포츠
음료
(Sports
Drinks)
CHIPS
NACHOS
BOMBAY MIX
NUTS
CANDY
CHOCOLATE
SPORTS DRINK
SODA
CORDIAL
COLA
POP
ICE TEA
탄산음료
(Soda)
아이스티
(Ice Tea)
음료수(Beverages)

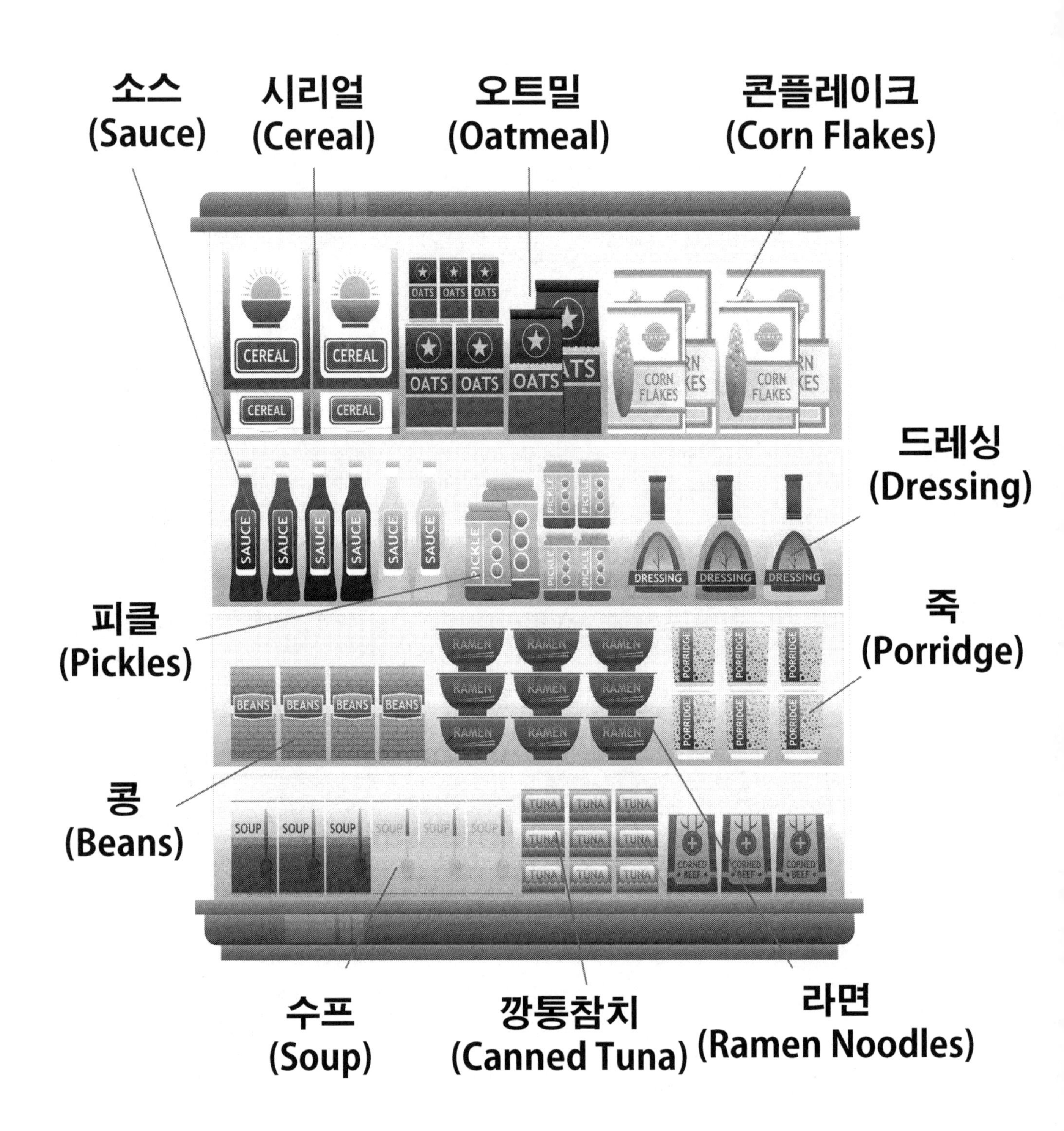
소스
(Sauce)
시리얼
(Cereal)
오트밀
(Oatmeal)
콘플레이크
(Corn Flakes)
드레싱
(Dressing)
피클
(Pickles)
죽
(Porridge)
콩
(Beans)
수프
(Soup)
깡통참치
(Canned Tuna)
라면
(Ramen Noodles)
CEREAL
OATS
CORN FLAKES
SAUCE
PICKLE
DRESSING
RAMEN
PORRIDGE
BEANS
SOUP
TUNA
CORNED BEEF

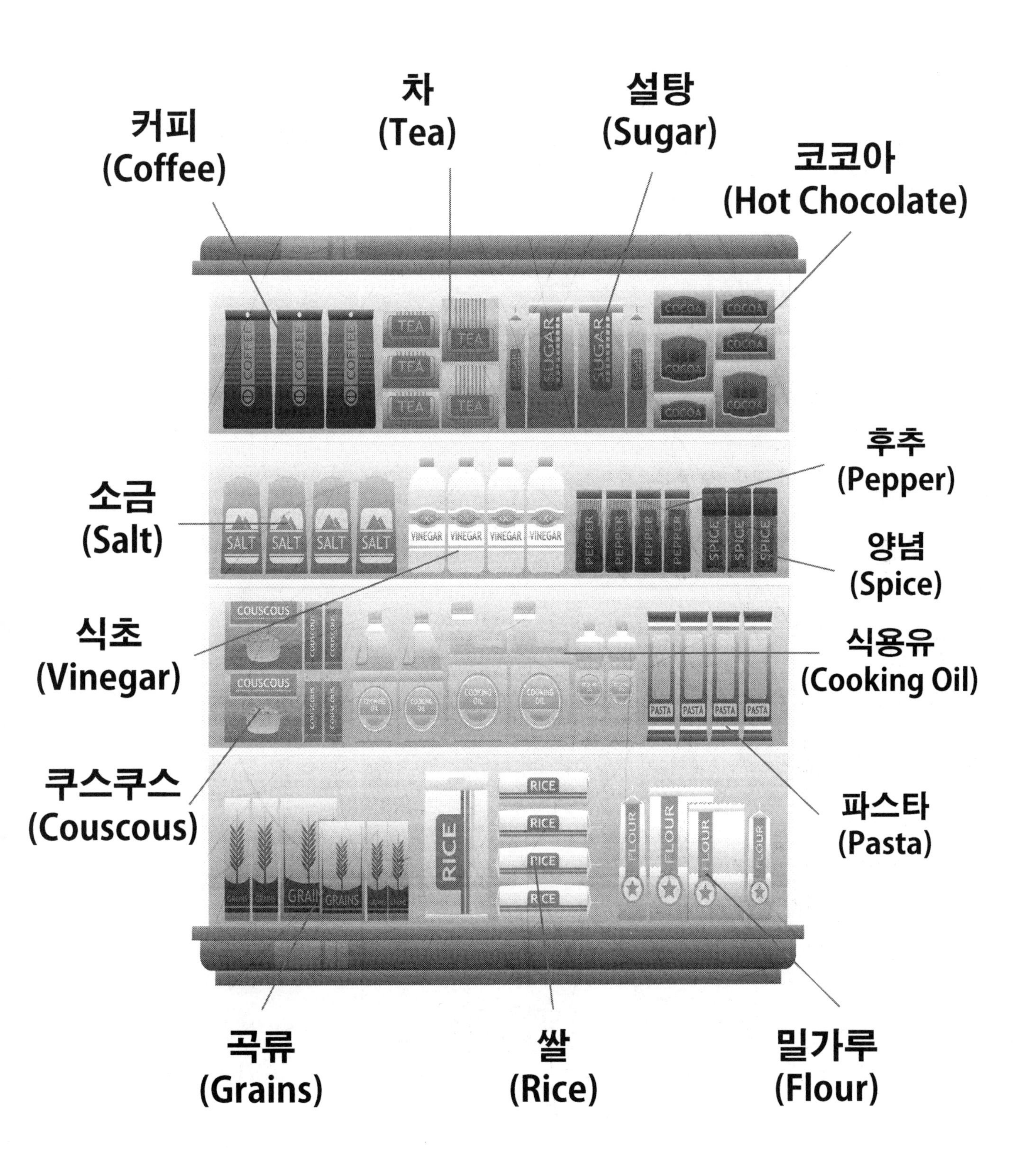

커피
(Coffee)
차
(Tea)
설탕
(Sugar)
코코아
(Hot Chocolate)
COFFEE
TEA
SUGAR
COCOA
후추
(Pepper)
소금
(Salt)
SALT
VINEGAR
PEPPER
SPICE
양념
(Spice)
식초
(Vinegar)
COUSCOUS
식용유
(Cooking Oil)
COOKING OIL
PASTA
쿠스쿠스
(Couscous)
RICE
FLOUR
GRAINS
파스타
(Pasta)
곡류
(Grains)
쌀
(Rice)
밀가루
(Flour)

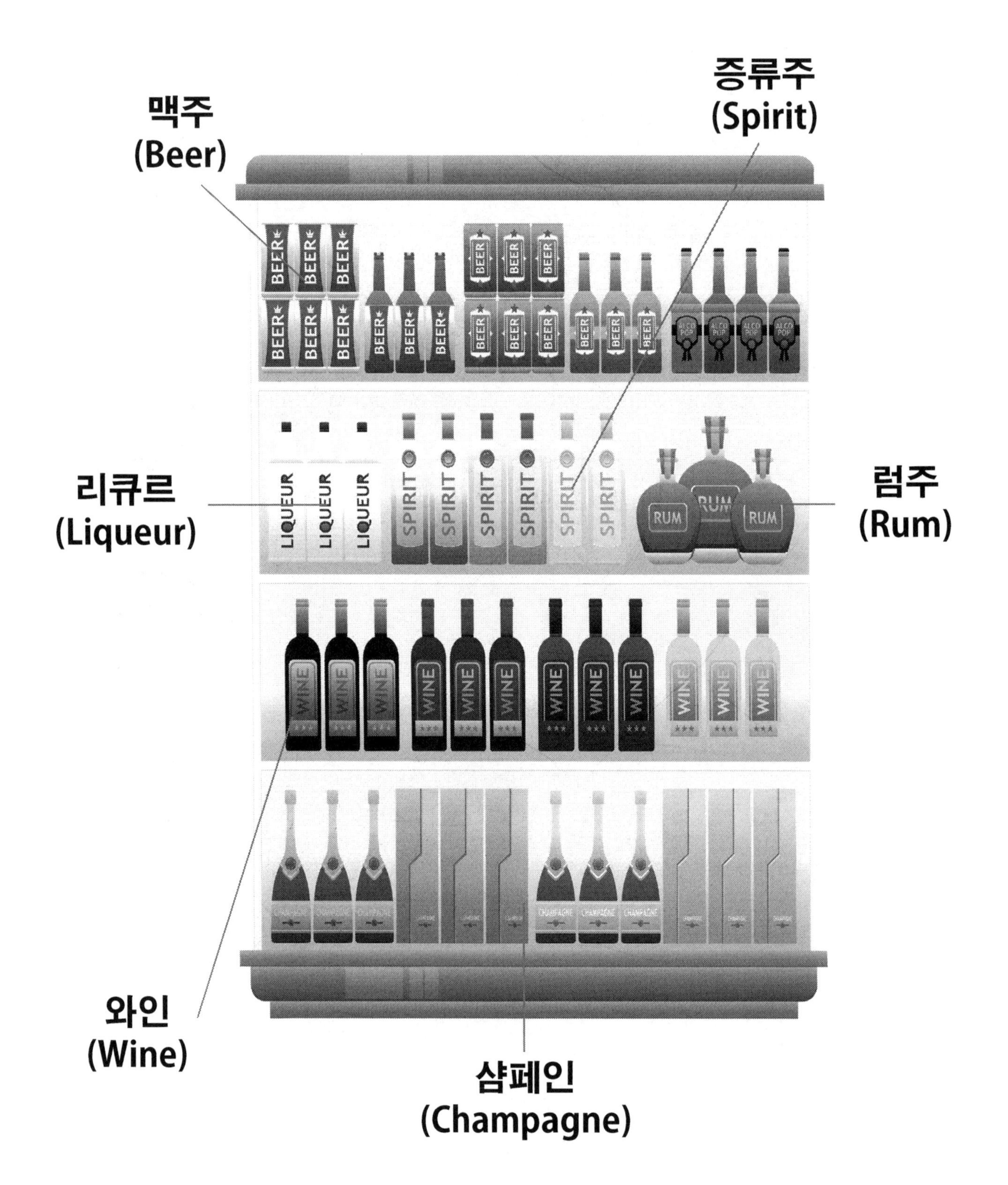
증류주
(Spirit)
맥주
(Beer)
BEER
ALCO POP
리큐르
(Liqueur)
LIQUEUR
SPIRIT
RUM
럼주
(Rum)
WINE
CHAMPAGNE
와인
(Wine)
샴페인
(Champagne)

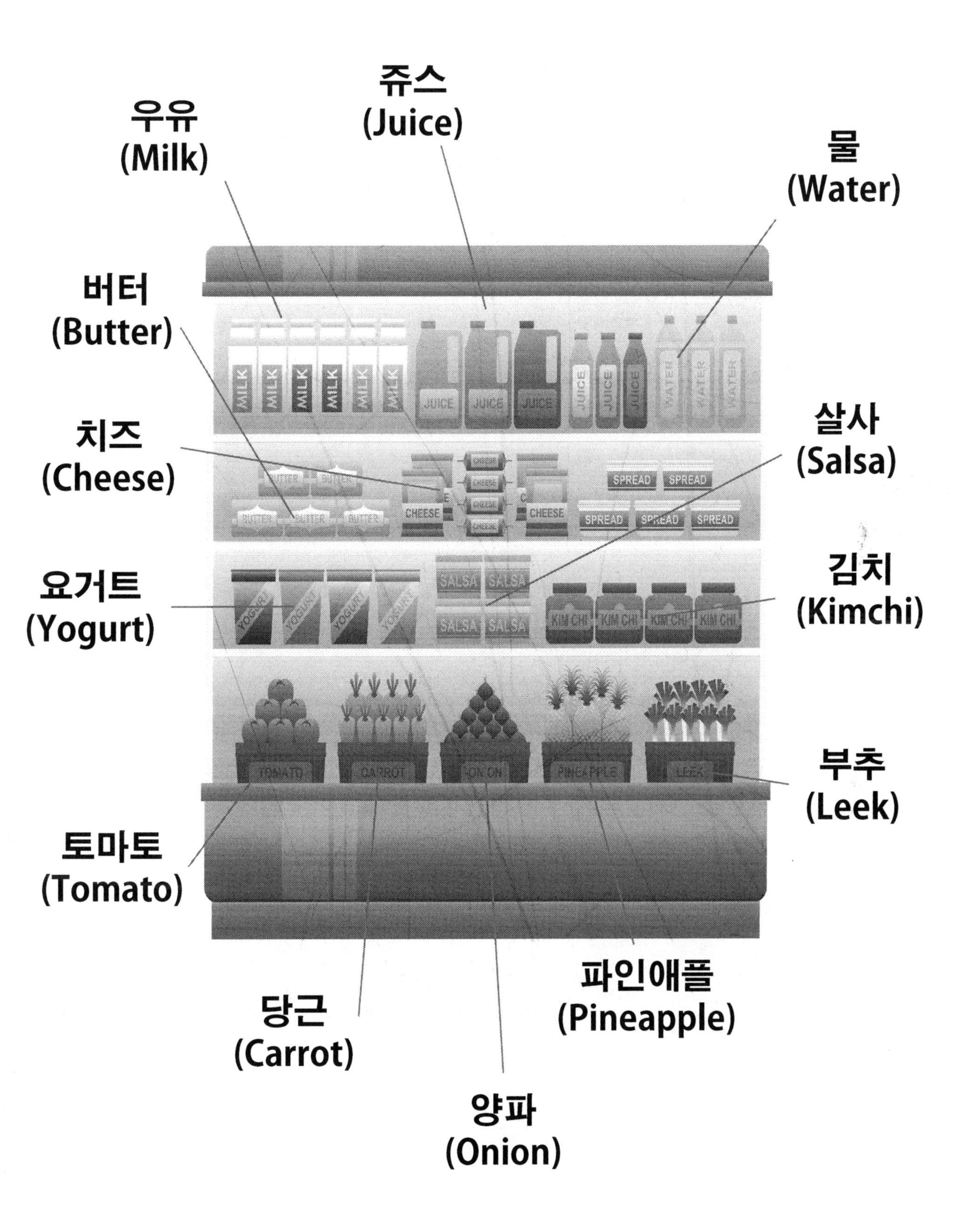
쥬스
(Juice)
우유
(Milk)
물
(Water)
버터
(Butter)
MILK
MILK
MILK
MILK
MILK
MILK
JUICE
JUICE
JUICE
JUICE
JUICE
JUICE
WATER
WATER
WATER
치즈
(Cheese)
살사
(Salsa)
BUTTER
BUTTER
BUTTER
BUTTER
BUTTER
CHEESE
CHEESE
SPREAD
SPREAD
SPREAD
SPREAD
SPREAD
김치
(Kimchi)
요거트
(Yogurt)
YOGURT
YOGURT
YOGURT
YOGURT
SALSA
SALSA
SALSA
SALSA
KIM CHI
KIM CHI
KIM CHI
KIM CHI
부추
(Leek)
TOMATO
CARROT
ONION
PINEAPPLE
LEEK
토마토
(Tomato)
파인애플
(Pineapple)
당근
(Carrot)
양파
(Onion)

EXPRESSIONS(표현)

벌꿀은 상하지 않는다
Honey never goes bad.

마요네즈 너무 많이 먹으면 살쪄.
Eating too much mayonnaise will make you fat.

사탕 너무 많이 먹으면 충치 생긴다.
Eating too much candy will give you cavities.

견과류는 건강에 아주 좋다.
Nuts are very good for health.

한국사람들은 오트밀 잘 안먹는다.
Korean people don`t enjoy oatmeal that much.

하지만, 죽은 아주 좋아한다.
But they love porridge.

라면은 더욱 좋아한다.
They love ramen noodles even more.

소금은 조금, 후추는 많이.
Little salt, lots of pepper.

코코아 한잔 마시자.
Let`s have a cup of hot chocolate.

맥주보다는 와인이 더 좋아.
I prefer wine to beer.

PEOPLE(사람)

소방관 (Firefighter)

우체부 (Mailman)

경찰관 (Police Officer)

목수 (Carpenter)

음악가 (Musician)

가수 (Singer)

기술자 (Engineer)

과학자 (Scientist)

의사 (Doctor)

요리사 (Chef)

미용사 (Hairdresser)

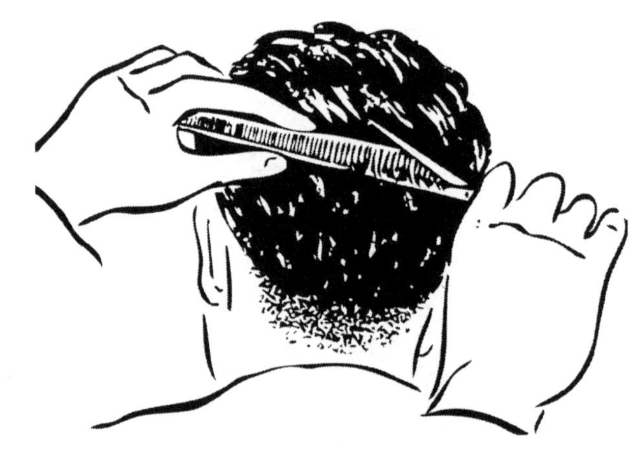

이발사 (Barber)

선생님 (Teacher)

학생 (Student)

사진사 (Photographer)

어부 (Fisherman)

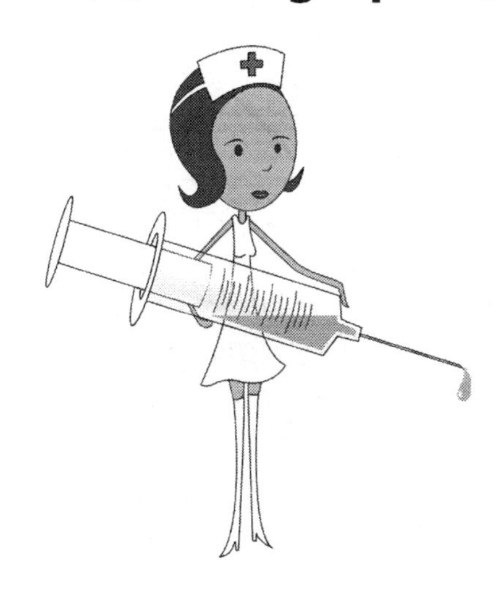

간호사 (Nurse)

연기자 (Actor)

재단사 (Tailor)

농부 (Farmer)

배관공 (Plumber)

경비원 (Security)

운동선수 (Athlete)

주부 (Housewife)

EXPRESSIONS(표현)

농부 없이는 음식도 없다.
Without a farmer there is no food.

경비원이 침입자를 저지했다.
The security stopped the intruder.

슈퍼마리오가 배관공이라는 것을 알고있니?
Did you know that Super Mario was a plumber?

주부는 가장 바쁜 직업중의 하나이다.
Housewife is one of the busiest jobs.

간호사도 의사만큼 중요하다.
Nurses are as important as doctors.

요리사 기분이 좋아야 음식 맛도 좋다.
Happy chef makes delicious meals.

우리 선생님은 모르는게 없다.
Our teacher knows everything.

어부는 물고기를 하나도 낚지 못했다.
The fisherman didn`t catch any fish.

미용사는 손재주가 필요하다.
Hairdressers need lots of dexterity.

너도 연습 많이 하면 가수가 될 수 있어.
You can also become a singer if you practice hard.

FAMILY(가족)

엄마 (Mom)
어머니 (Mother)

아빠 (Dad)
아버지 (Father)

할머니 (Grandma)

할아버지 (Grandpa)

형 (Male to Male)
오빠 (Female to Male)
(Older Brother)

언니 (Female to Female)
누나 (Male to Female)
(Older Sister)

동생 (Younger Sibling)

여동생: younger sister
남동생: younger brother

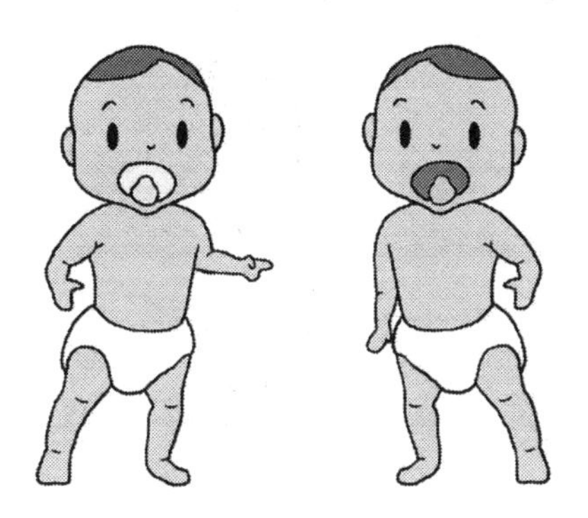

쌍둥이 (Twins) (쌍동이)
세쌍둥이 (Triplet) (세쌍동이)

부부 (Husband and Wife)

이모 (Aunt)

Mother's sister

고모
Father's sister

삼촌 (Uncle) on Father's side

외삼촌 Uncle on Mother's side

아기 (Baby) / 아깨 / 개

EXPRESSIONS(표현)

동생에게 잘 해줘라.
Be nice to your younger brother/sister.

아빠는 아직까지 자고있다.
Dad is still sleeping

엄마는 설거지 하느라 바쁘다.
Mom is busy doing the dishes.

누나는 KPOP을 좋아한다.
My older sister likes KPOP.

우리 할머니는 재미있는 이야기를 많이 아신다..
My grandma knows lots of fun stories.

우리 할아버지는 야구를 좋아하신다.
My grandpa likes baseball.

우리 이모는 아주 멋쟁이다.
My aunt is very fashionable.

우리 삼촌은 비디오게임을 좋아한다.
My uncle likes video games.

아기가 태어났다.
A baby is born.

부부는 엄마와 아빠를 뜻한다.
Husband and wife mean mom and dad.

EMOTIONS(감정)

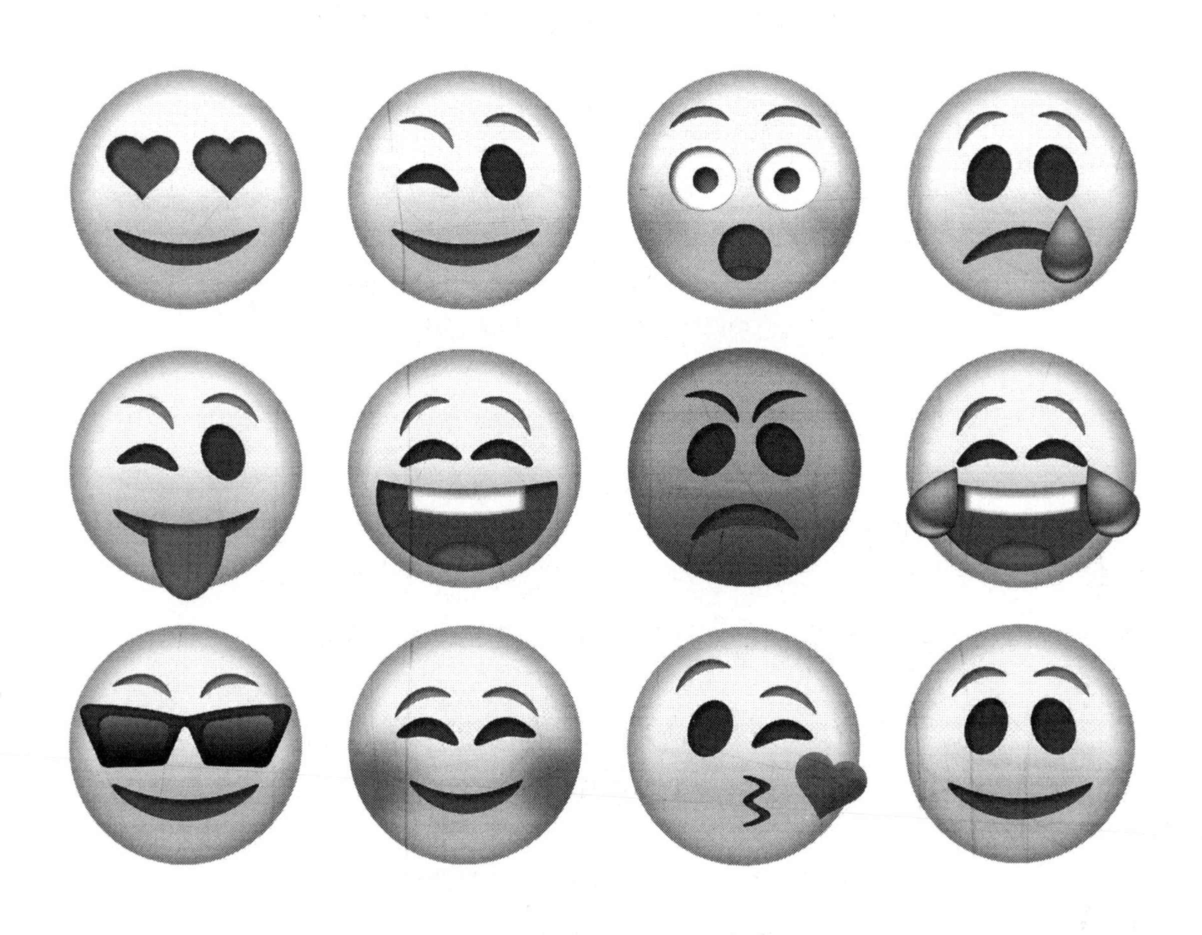

사랑에 빠진 (In Love)	장난기있는 (Playful)	놀란 (Surprised)	슬픈 (Sad)
익살스러운 (Comical)	행복한 (Happy)	화난 (Angry)	기뻐하는 (Joyful)
자신있는 (Confident)	수줍은 (Shy)	매력있는 (Charming)	평온한 (Calm)

EXPRESSIONS(표현)

사랑에 빠진 사람.
A person who is in love.

익살스러운 얼굴.
A comical face.

자신있는 발언.
A confident statement.

장난기있는 강아지.
A playful puppy.

행복한 인생.
A happy life.

수줍은 여자 아이.
A shy little girl.

놀란 모습.
Looking surprised.

화난 목소리.
An angry voice.

매력있는 성격.
A charming personality.

매우 평온한 아침.
A very calm morning.

TRANSPORTATION(교통)

내비게이션
(Navigation)

송풍구
(Air Vent)

계기판
(Dashboard)

비상등
(Emergency Light)

룸미러
(Rearview Mirror)

사이드미러
(Side Mirror)

에어백
(Airbags)

변속기
(Gearbox)

경적
(Horn)

운전대
(Streering Wheel)

조수석
(Passenger Seat)

방향지시등
(Turn Signal)

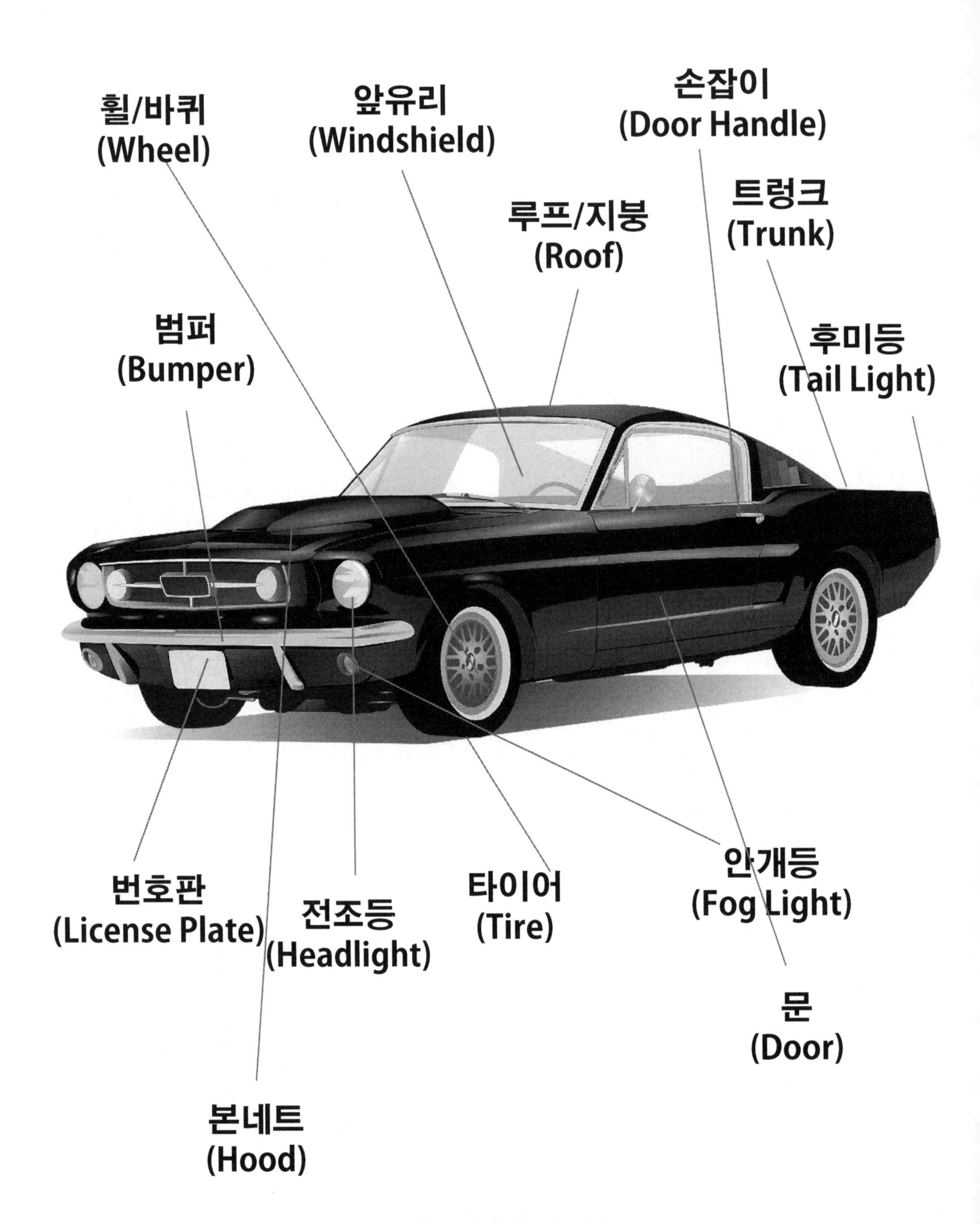

휠/바퀴
(Wheel)
앞유리
(Windshield)
손잡이
(Door Handle)
트렁크
(Trunk)
루프/지붕
(Roof)
범퍼
(Bumper)
후미등
(Tail Light)
번호판
(License Plate)
전조등
(Headlight)
타이어
(Tire)
안개등
(Fog Light)
문
(Door)
본네트
(Hood)

비행기 (Airplane)

버스 (Bus)

자전거 (Bicycle)

오토바이 (Motorcycle)

기차 (Train)

지하철 (Subway)

헬리콥터 (Helicopter)

고속버스 (Express Bus)

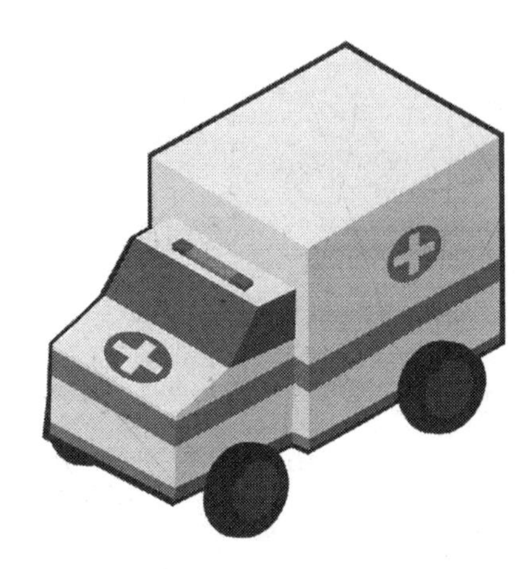

구급차 (Ambulance)

배 (Ship)

택시 (Taxi)

요트 (Yacht)

선장 (Captain of a Ship)

기장 (Pilot)

운전사 (Driver)

기관사 (Train Engineer)

선원 (Sailor)

승무원 (Flight Attendant)

탑승객 (Passenger)

기내식 (In-Flight Meal)

구명조끼 (Life Vest)

비상구 (Emergency Exit)

계단 (Stairs)

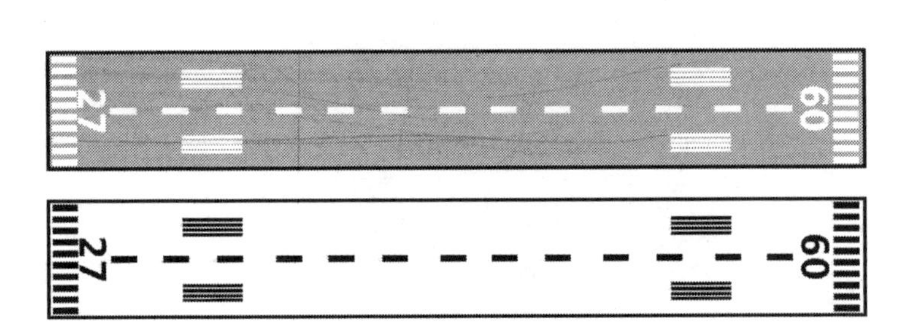

활주로 (Runway)

수하물 (Luggage)

자물쇠 (Lock)

보안요원 (Security)

탑승권 (Boarding Pass)

여권 (Passport)

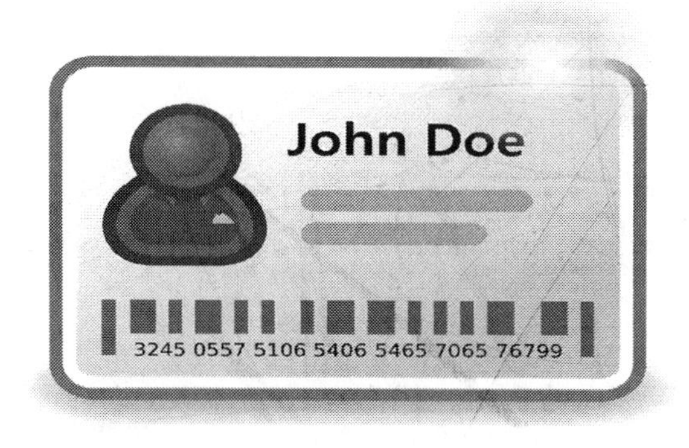

신분증 (Identification Card)

EXPRESSIONS(표현)

수하물은 몇개까지 허용되나요?
How many luggage are allowed?

탑승권을 보여주세요.
Show be the boarding pass, please.

당신 여권이 만료되었네요.
Your passport has expired.

기내식을 너무 많이 먹었어요.
I ate too much in-flight meal.

비상구의 위치를 확인하세요.
Please check the location of the emergency exit.

경험많은 기장.
A seasoned pilot.

승무원의 지시를 따르세요.
Listen to what the flight attendant says.

구급차에게 양보하세요.
Please yield to an ambulance.

지하철은 매우 안정적인 교통수단이다.
Subway is a very stable means of transportation.

오토바이는 위험하다.
Motorcycles are dangerous.

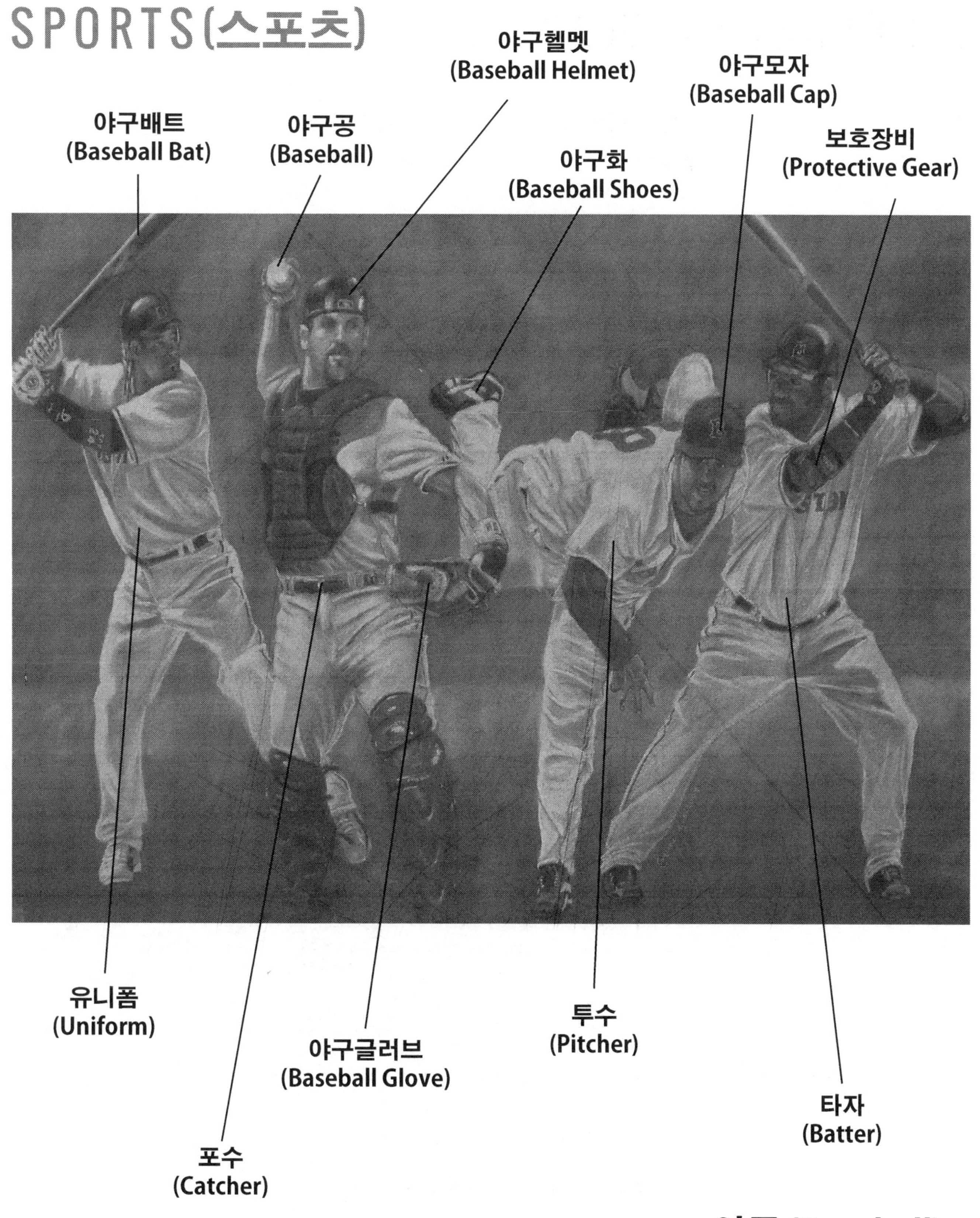
야구헬멧
(Baseball Helmet)
야구모자
(Baseball Cap)
야구배트
(Baseball Bat)
야구공
(Baseball)
보호장비
(Protective Gear)
야구화
(Baseball Shoes)
유니폼
(Uniform)
야구글러브
(Baseball Glove)
투수
(Pitcher)
타자
(Batter)
포수
(Catcher)

야구 (Baseball)

축구 (Soccer)

배구 (Volleyball)

미식축구
(American Football)

아이스 하키 (Ice Hockey)

농구 (Basketball)

달리기 (Running)

양궁
(Archery)

권투 (Boxing)

경마 (Horse Racing)

탁구 (Table Tennis)

태권도 (Tae Kwon Do)

심판 (Referee)

경기장 (Stadium)

입장권
(Admission Ticket)

관중
(Audience)

시상대 (Winner`s Podium)

결승선 (Finish Line)

야구 배트 (Baseball Bat)

축구화 (Soccer Shoes)

트로피 (Trophy)

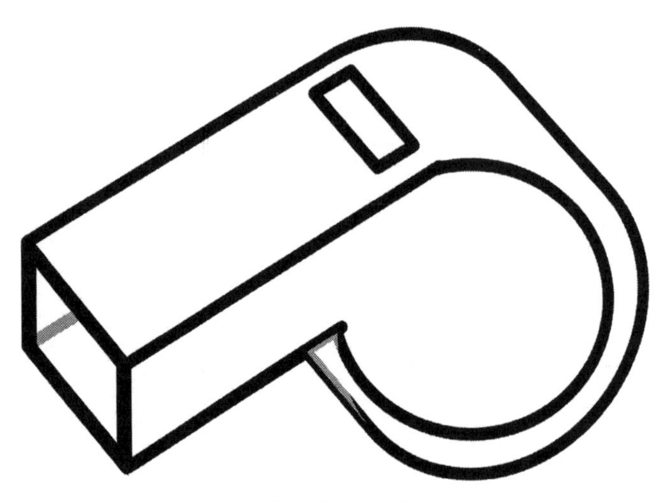

호루라기(Whistle)

운동복 (Jersey)

야구 글러브 (Baseball Glove)

줄넘기 (Jump Rope)

턱걸이 (Chin Up)

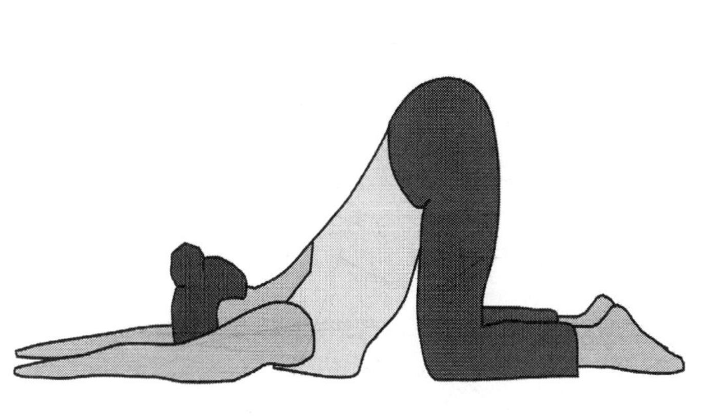

요가 (Yoga)

윗몸 일으키기 (Sit-Up)

러닝머신 (Treadmill)

EXPRESSIONS(표현)

축구는 세계적으로 인기있다.
Soccer is popular around the globe.

농구는 누구나 즐길 수 있는 운동이다.
Basketball is a sport which anybody can enjoy.

양궁은 집중력이 필요하다.
Archery requires lots of focus.

미식축구가 서서히 인기를 얻고 있다.
American football is slowly getting more popular.

권투는 살빼기에 효과적이다.
Boxing is effective for fat burning.

태권도는 한국의 전통 무예이다.
Taekwondo is traditional martial arts of Korea.

심판이 실수했다.
The referee made a mistake.

입장권이 왜 이렇게 비싸?
Why is the admission ticket so expensive?

경기장이 엄청나게 크다.
The stadium is gigantic.

결승선에 거의 다 왔다!
We are almost at the finish line!

ANIMALS(동물)

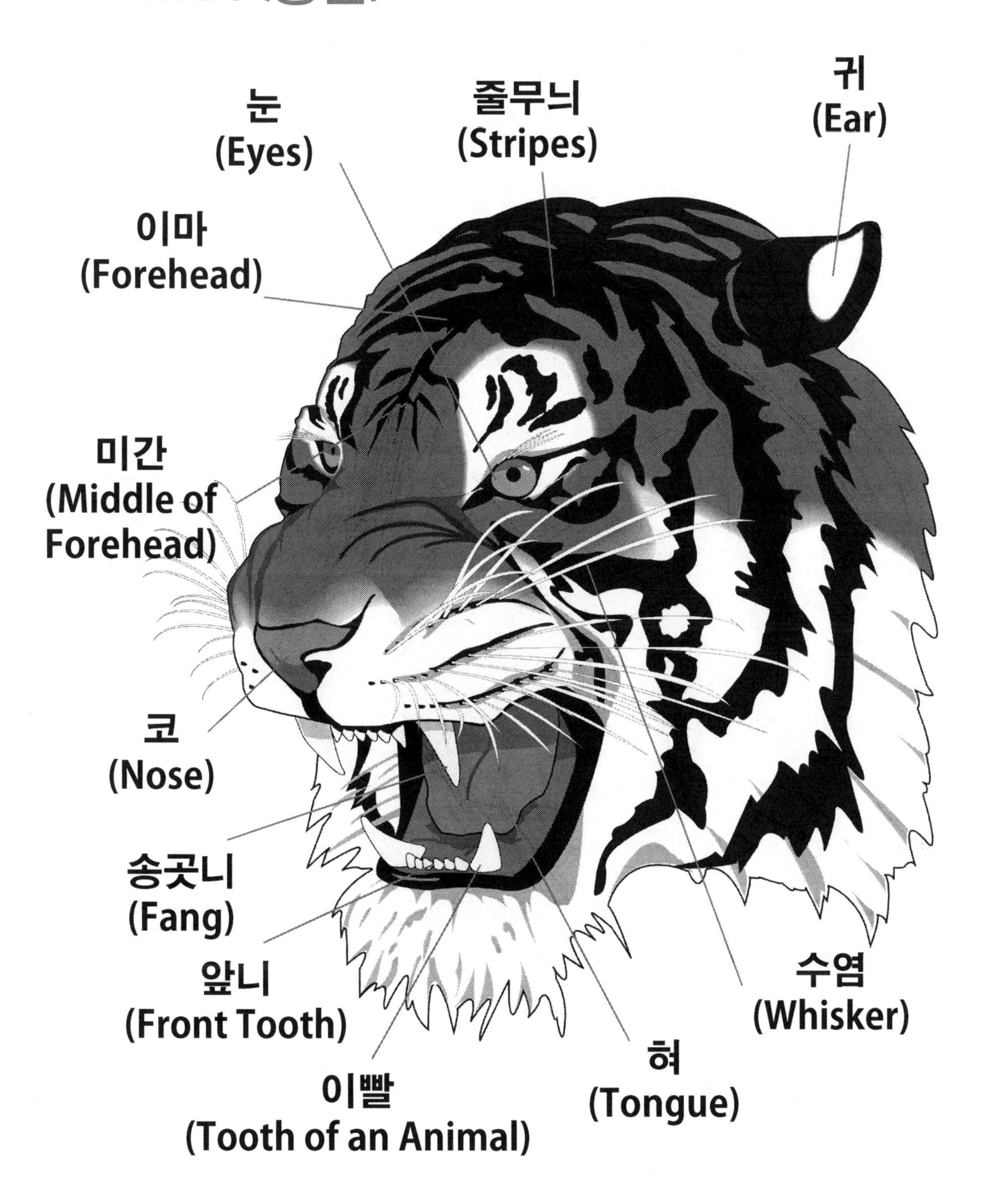
눈
(Eyes)
줄무늬
(Stripes)
귀
(Ear)
이마
(Forehead)
미간
(Middle of Forehead)
코
(Nose)
송곳니
(Fang)
앞니
(Front Tooth)
이빨
(Tooth of an Animal)
혀
(Tongue)
수염
(Whisker)

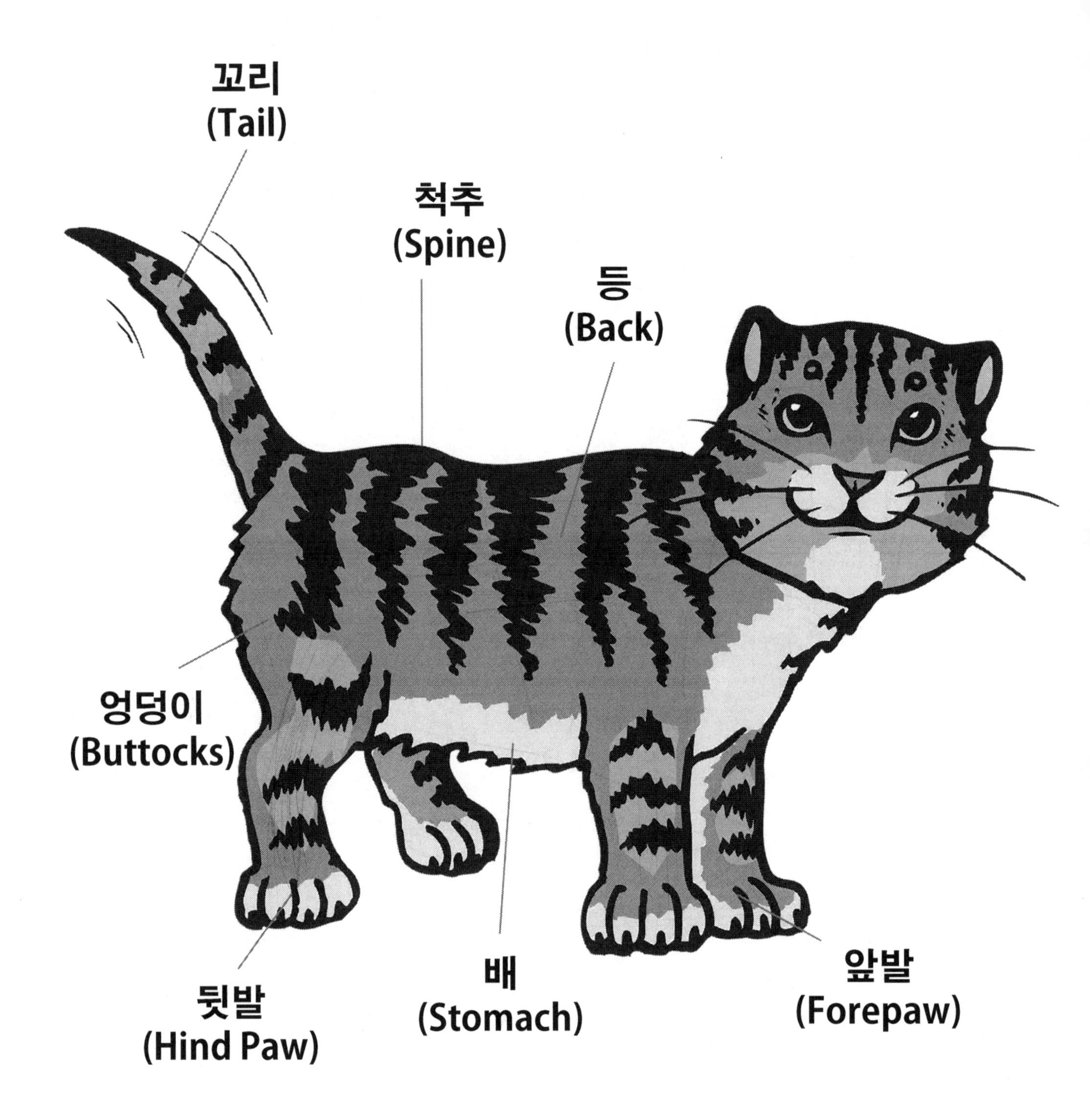
꼬리
(Tail)
척추
(Spine)
등
(Back)
엉덩이
(Buttocks)
뒷발
(Hind Paw)
배
(Stomach)
앞발
(Forepaw)

코끼리 (Elephant)

사자 (Lion)

코뿔소 (Rhinoceros)

기린 (Giraffe)

소 (Cow)

나무늘보 (Sloth)

양 (Sheep)

말 (Horse)

개 (Dog)
강아지 (Puppy)

고양이 (Cat)
새끼고양이 (Kitten)

하마 (Hippo)

토끼 (Rabbit)

영양 (Antelope)

쥐 (Mouse)

호랑이 (Tiger)

늑대 (Wolf)

사슴 (Deer)

원숭이 (Monkey)

표범 (Leopard)

얼룩말 (Zebra)

여우 (Fox)

고슴도치 (Hedgehog)

두더지 (Mole)

다람쥐 (Squirrel)

오소리 (Badger)

너구리 (Raccoon)

돌고래 (Dolphin)

수달 (Otter)

물개 (Seal)

곰 (Bear)

EXPRESSIONS(표현)

너구리가 내 점심을 훔쳤다.
A raccoon stole my lunch.

돌고래는 정말 귀엽다.
Dolphins are really cute.

수달은 정말 똑똑하다.
Otters are really smart.

얼룩말은 굉장히 다혈질이다.
Zebras are very hot-headed.

여우는 영악하다.
Foxes are sly.

호랑이는 무섭다.
Tigers are scary.

사슴은 아름답다.
Deer are gorgeous.

하마는 입이 크다.
Hippos have a huge mouth.

말은 굉장히 빠르다.
Horses are extremely fast.

기린은 정말 키가 크다.
Giraffes are really tall.

BIRDS(새/조류)

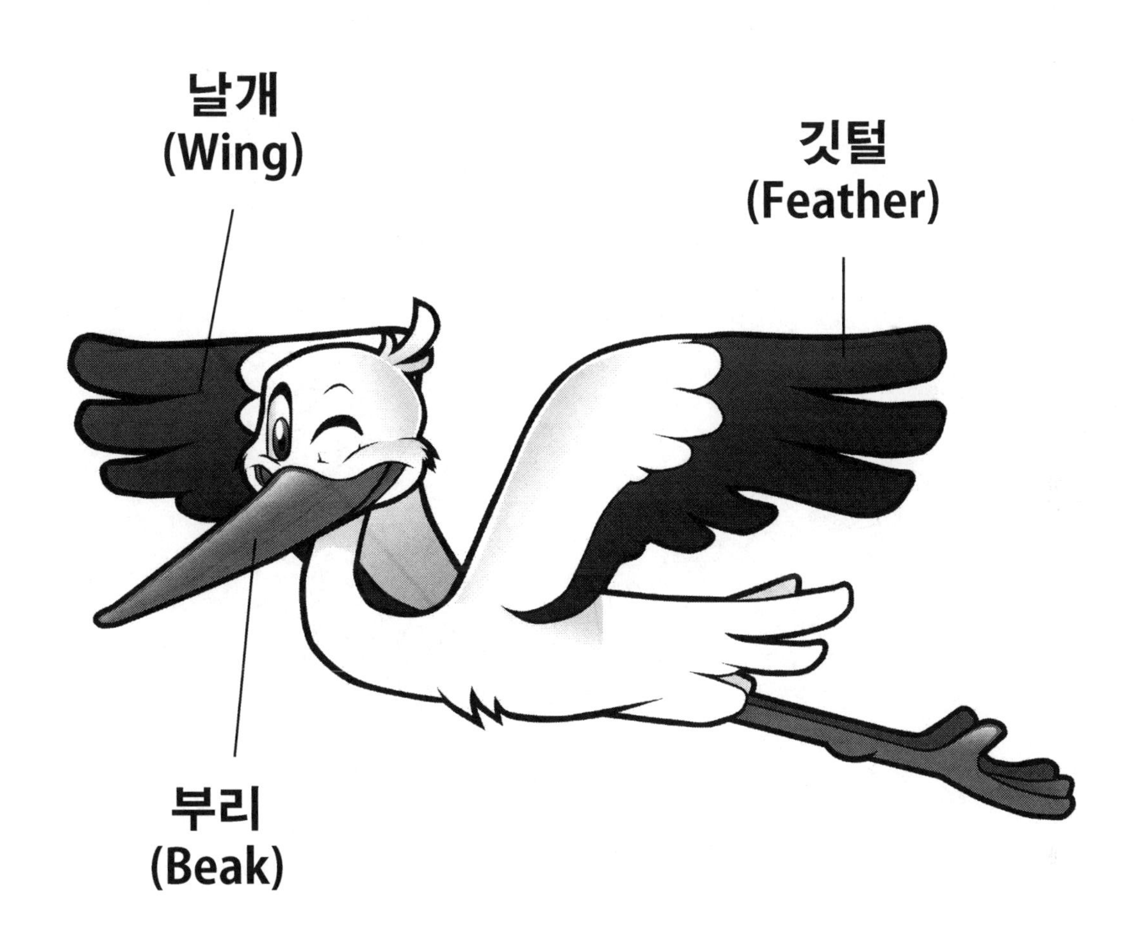

닭 (Chicken)

오리 (Duck)

거위 (Goose)

독수리 (Eagle)

앵무새 (Parrot)

올빼미 (Owl)

두루미 (Crane)

백조 (Swan)

갈매기 (Gull)

타조 (Ostrich)

펭귄 (Penguin)

까마귀 (Crow)

공작새 (Peacock)

칠면조 (Turkey)

파랑새 (Bluebird)

참새 (Sparrow)

매 (Hawk)

황새 (Stork)

EXPRESSIONS(표현)

공작새는 굉장히 화려하다.
Peacocks are very colorful.

펭귄도 새야?
Is penguin a bird?

올빼미는 잠을 안자나?
Don`t owls ever sleep?

앵무새는 사람 흉내를 잘낸다.
Parrots are good at mimicking human sounds.

백조의 호수
Swan Lake

타조는 정말 빠르다.
Ostriches are really fast.

오리는 뒤뚱거린다.
Ducks waddle.

닭은 사회적인 동물이라고 한다.
It is said that chickens are social animals.

독수리는 용맹하다.
Eagles are brave.

깃털처럼 가볍다.
Light as a feather.

INSECTS(곤충)

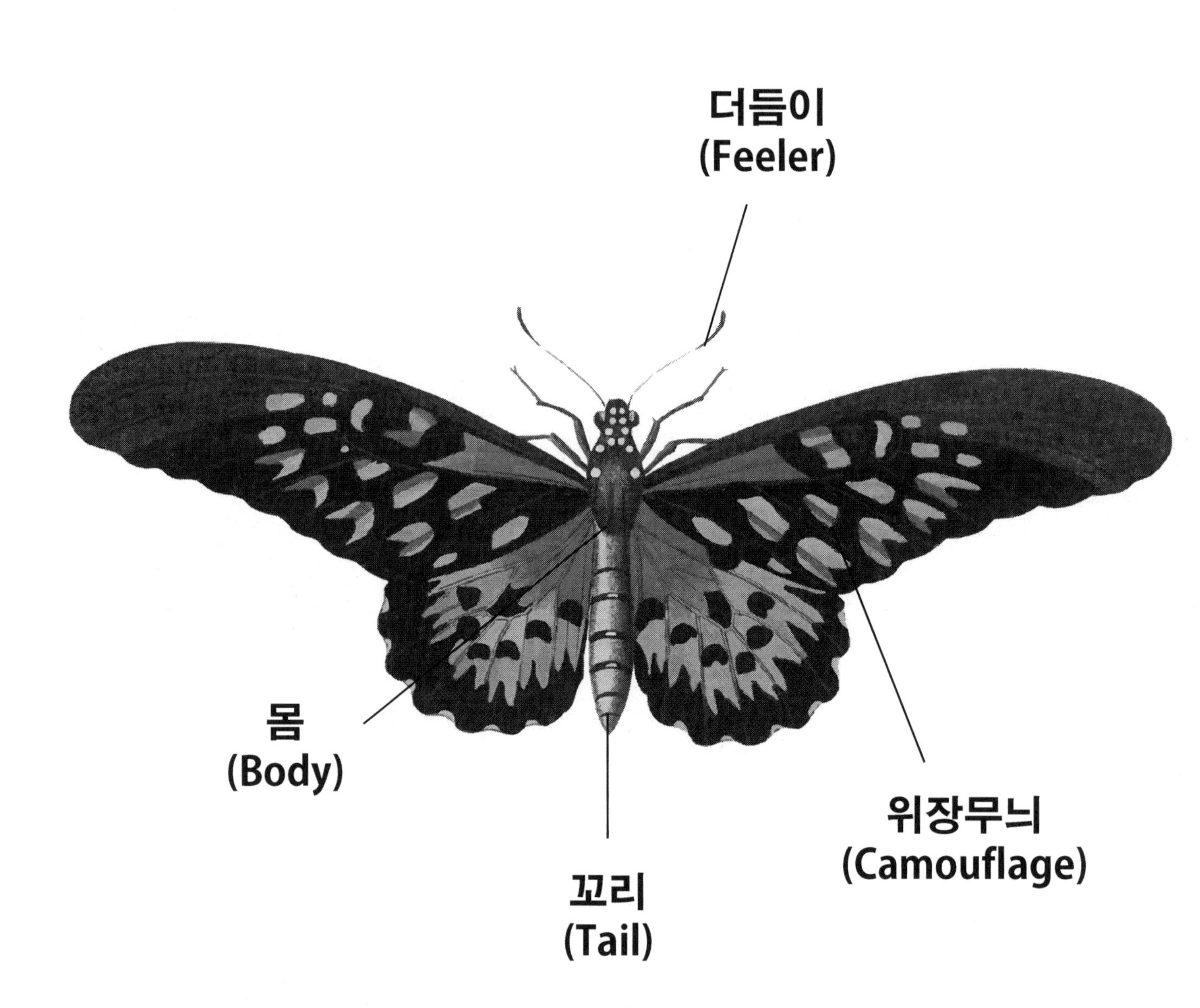

나비
(Butterfly)

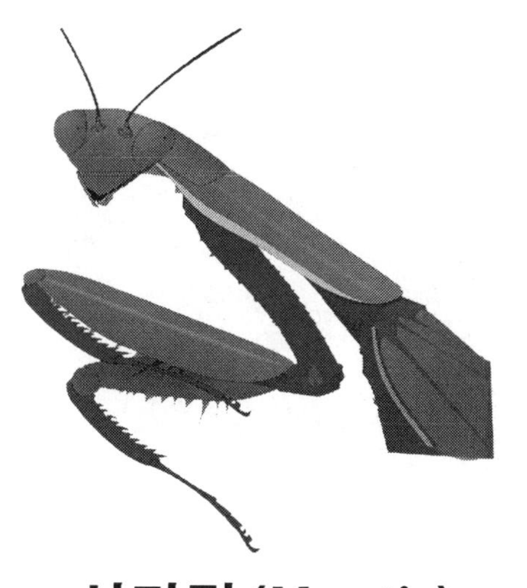

사마귀 (Mantis)

개미 (Ant)

잠자리 (Dragonfly)

나방 (Moth)

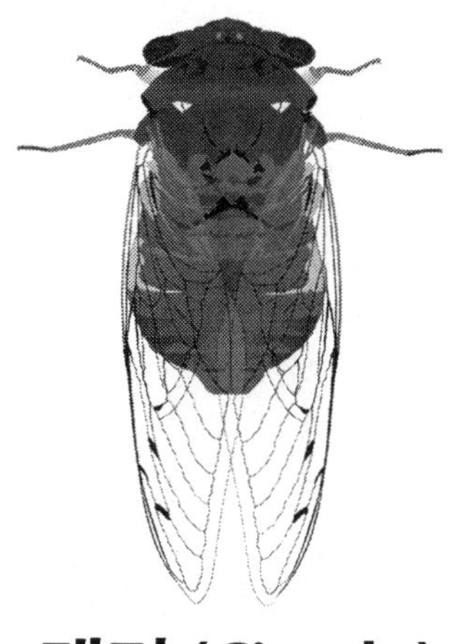

매미 (Cicada)

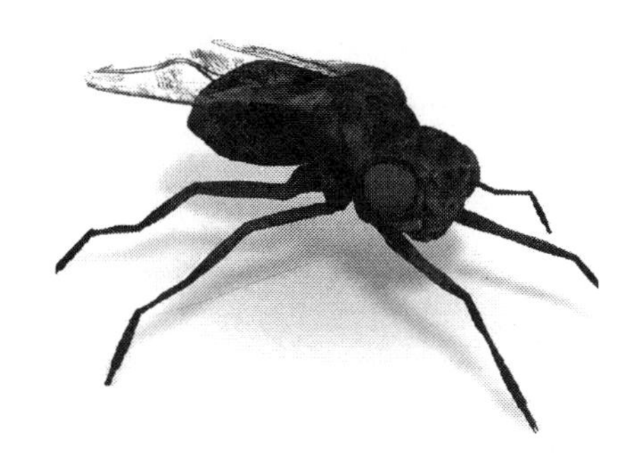

파리 (Fly)

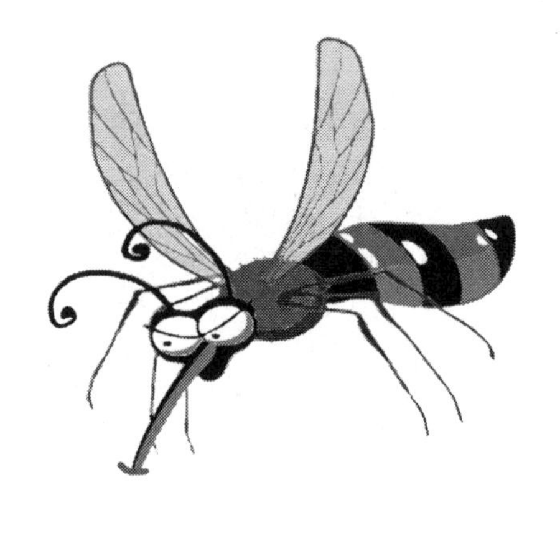

모기 (Mosquito)

무당벌레 (Ladybug)

벌 (Bee)

말벌 (Wasp)

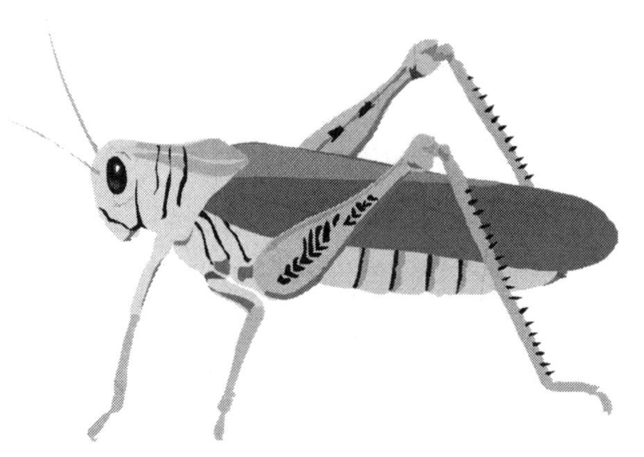

메뚜기 (Grasshopper)

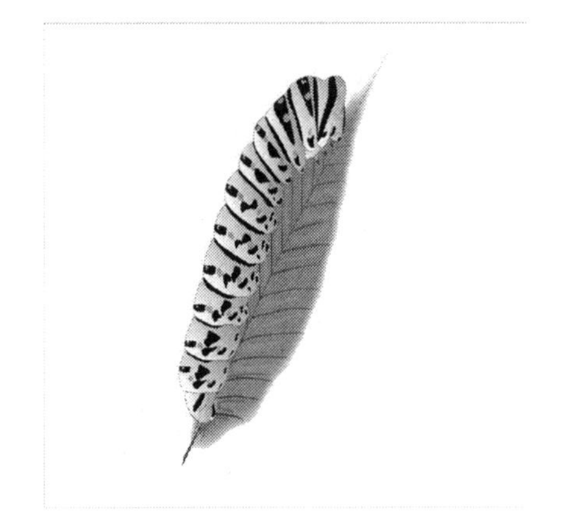

애벌레 (Larva)

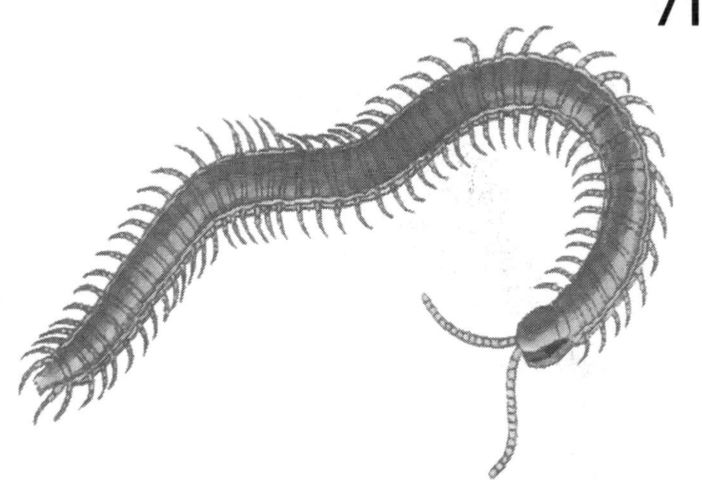

지네 (Centipede)

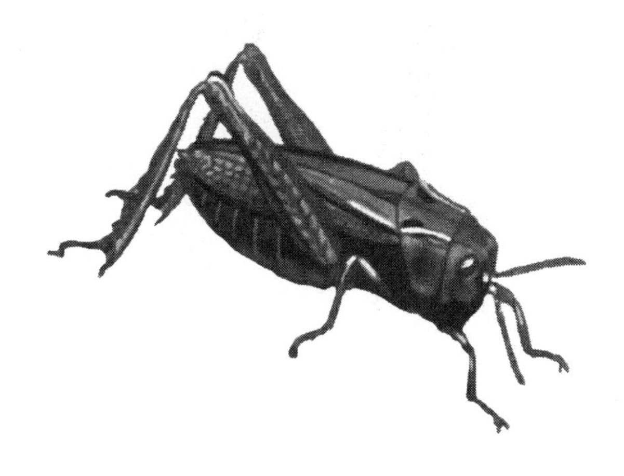

귀뚜라미 (Cricket)

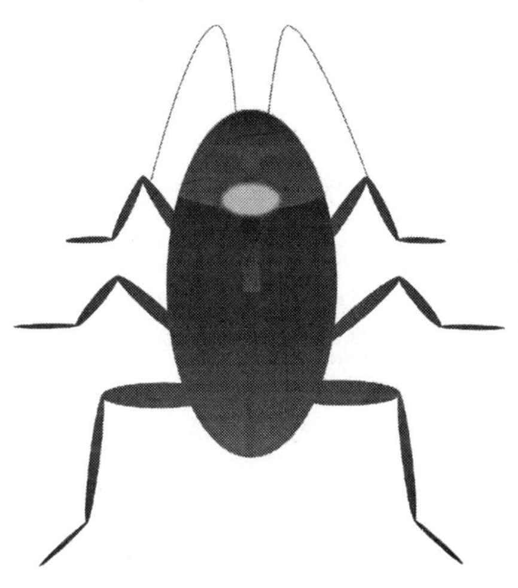

바퀴벌레 (Roach)

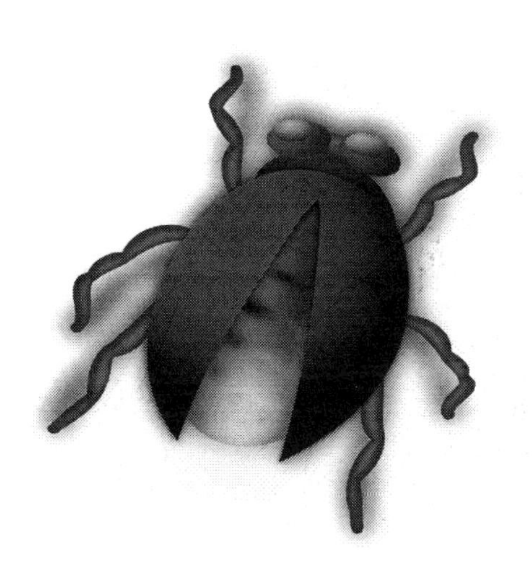

개똥벌레 (Firefly)

풍뎅이 (Beetle)

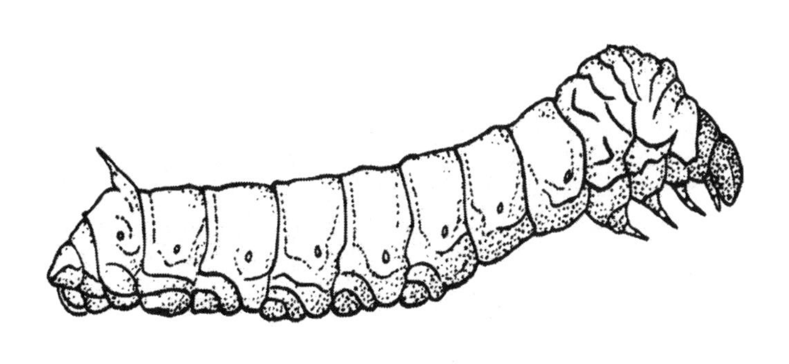

누에 (Silkworm)

EXPRESSIONS(표현)

나방은 나비와 매우 비슷하다.
Moths are very similar to butterflies.

잠자리는 해충을 잡아먹는다.
Dragonflies eat harmful insects.

매미는 여름에 정말 시끄럽다.
Cicadas are really noisy in the summer.

파리는 정말 성가시다.
Flies are so annoying.

모기때문에 잠을 못잤다!
Mosquitoes kept me up all night!

말벌은 정말 무서워.
Wasps are really scary.

벌이 없으면 꿀도 없다.
No bees, no honey.

무당벌레는 행운의 상징이다.
Ladybugs are a symbol of good luck.

바퀴벌레는 정말 역겨워.
Roaches are really disgusting.

개똥벌레의 빛
The glow of a firefly

FISH / MARINE LIFE (물고기/해양생물)

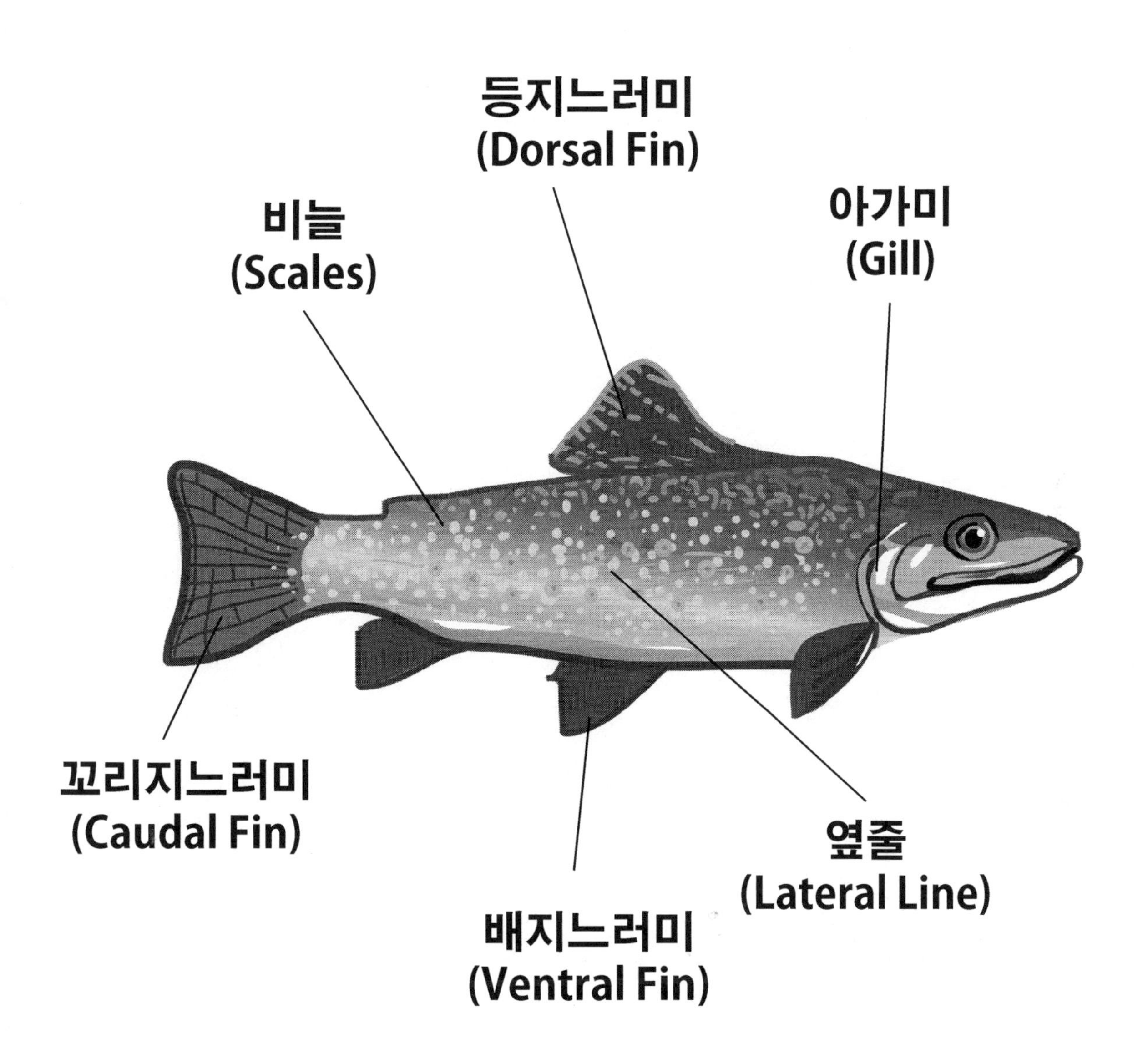

상어 (Shark)

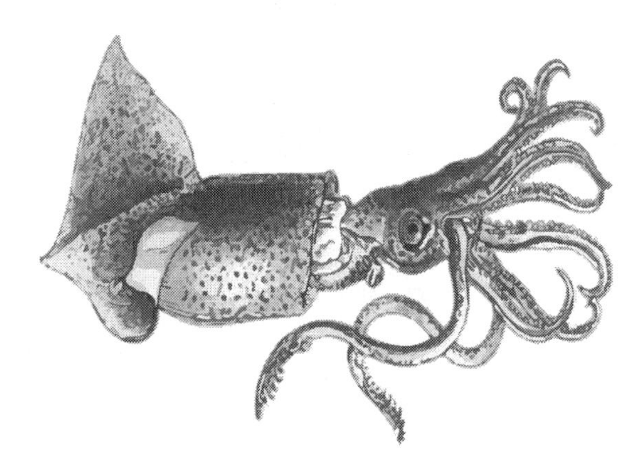

오징어 (Squid)

문어 (Octopus)

잉어 (Carp)

불가사리 (Starfish)

해파리 (Jellyfish)

해마 (Sea Horse)

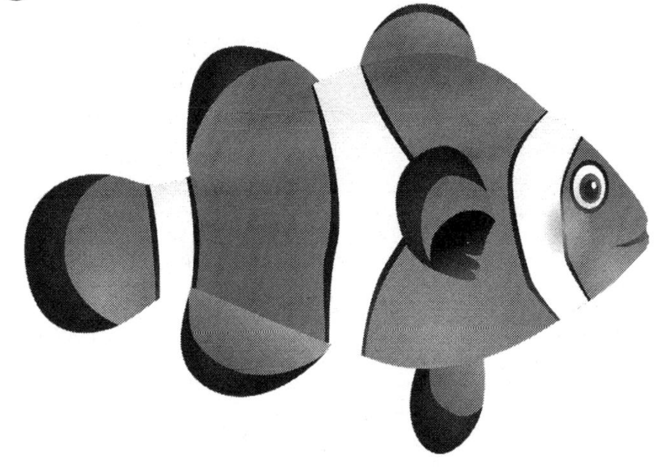

열대어 (Tropical Fish)

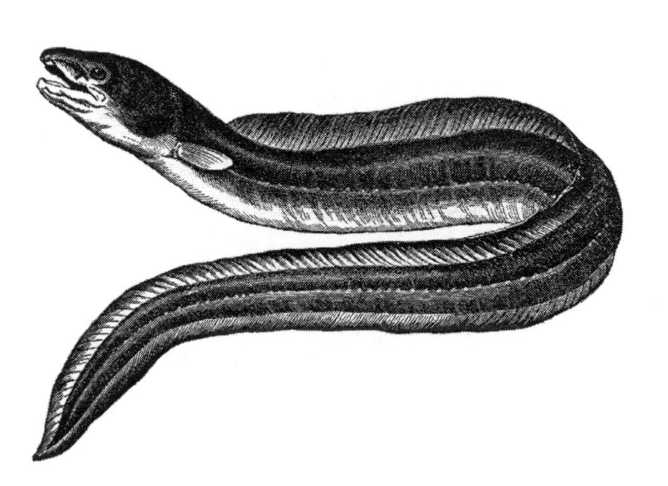

장어 (Eel)

참치 (Tuna)

거북이 (Turtle)

소라 (Conch)

민물가재 (Crawfish)

새우 (Shrimp)

해초 (Seaweed)

산호 (Coral)

황새치 (Swordfish)

굴 (Oyster)

EXPRESSIONS(표현)

물고기는 아가미로 숨쉰다.
Fish breathe through their gills.

상어는 포식자이다.
Sharks are predators.

구운 오징어는 맛있다.
Grilled squid tastes good.

문어는 다리가 8개이다.
An octopus has eight legs.

해마는 동물같이 생겼다.
Sea horses look like an animal.

열대어는 정말 화려하다.
Tropical fish are really colorful.

거북이는 느리다.
Turtles are slow.

새우는 영양소가 풍부하다.
Shrimps are nutritious.

산호는 바다의 꽃이다.
Corals are the flowers of the sea.

굴에는 아연이 풍부하다.
Oysters are a good source of zinc.

REPTILES/AMPHIBIANS(파충류/양서류)

도마뱀 (Lizard)

뱀 (Snake)

악어 (Alligator)

카멜레온 (Chameleon)

두꺼비 (Toad)

개구리 (Frog)

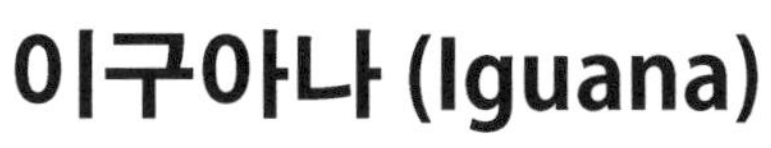

이구아나 (Iguana)

공룡 (Dinosaur)

방울뱀 (Rattlesnake)

도롱뇽 (Salamander)

코브라 (Cobra)

EXPRESSIONS(표현)

나는 애완용으로 도마뱀을 기른다.
I keep a lizard as a pet.

뱀은 독이있다.
Snakes are venomous.

악어는 입이 크다.
Alligators have a huge mouth.

카멜레온의 진짜 색은 무엇일까?
What is the real color of a chameleon?

두꺼비는 못생겼다.
Toads are ugly.

개구리는 귀엽다.
Frogs are cute.

방울뱀을보면 도망가라!.
When you see a rattlesnake, run away!

공룡은 멸종했다.
Dinosaurs went extinct.

이구아나는 무엇을 먹지?
What do iguanas eat?

코브라는 뱀중에서 가장 무섭다.
Cobras are the scariest among all snakes.

PLANTS/FRUITS/NUTS / VEGETABLES (식물/과일/견과류/야채)

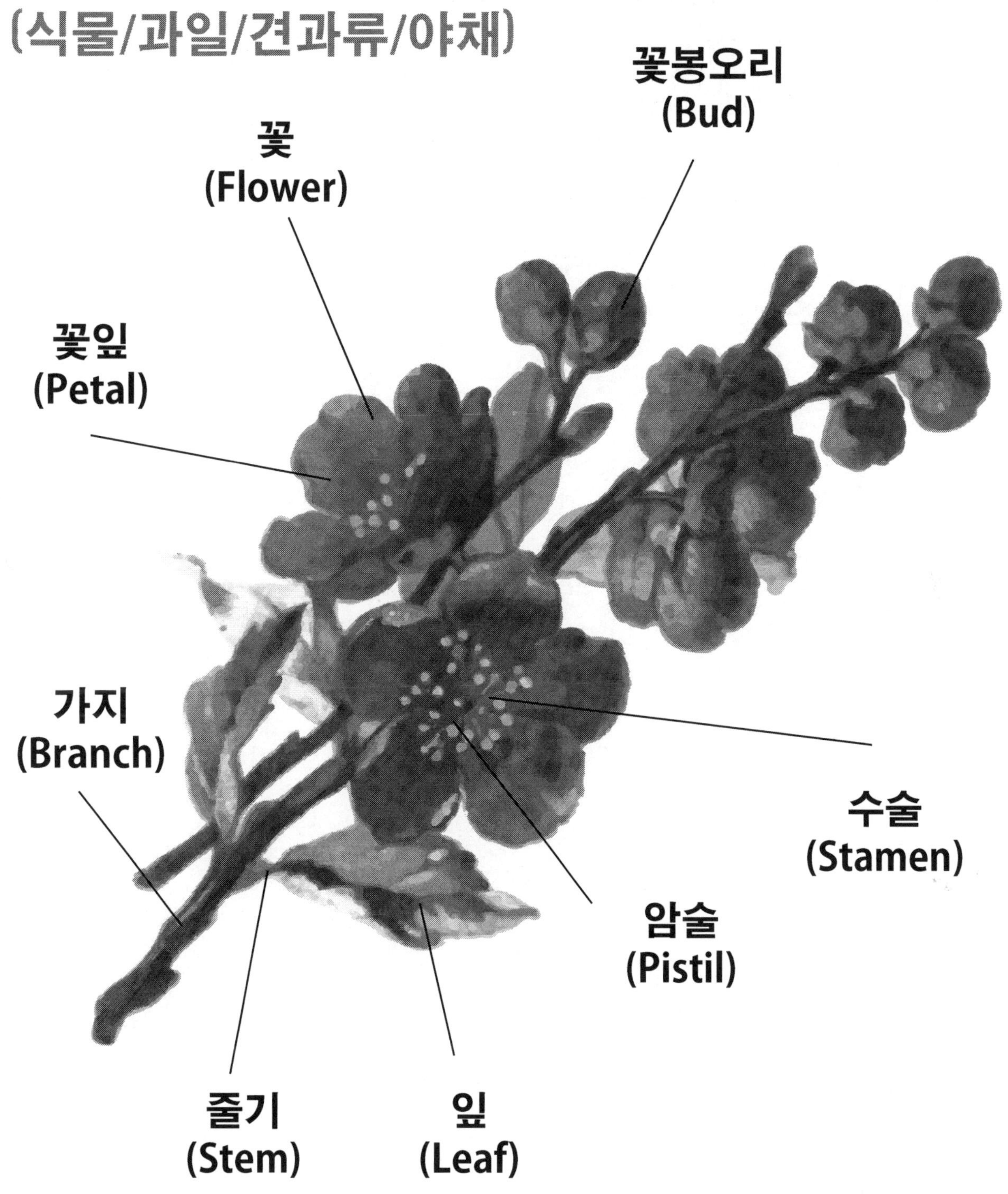

장미 (Rose)

해바라기 (Sunflower)

선인장 (Cactus)

벚꽃 (Cherry Blossoms)

연꽃 (Lotus)

나팔꽃 (Morning Glory)

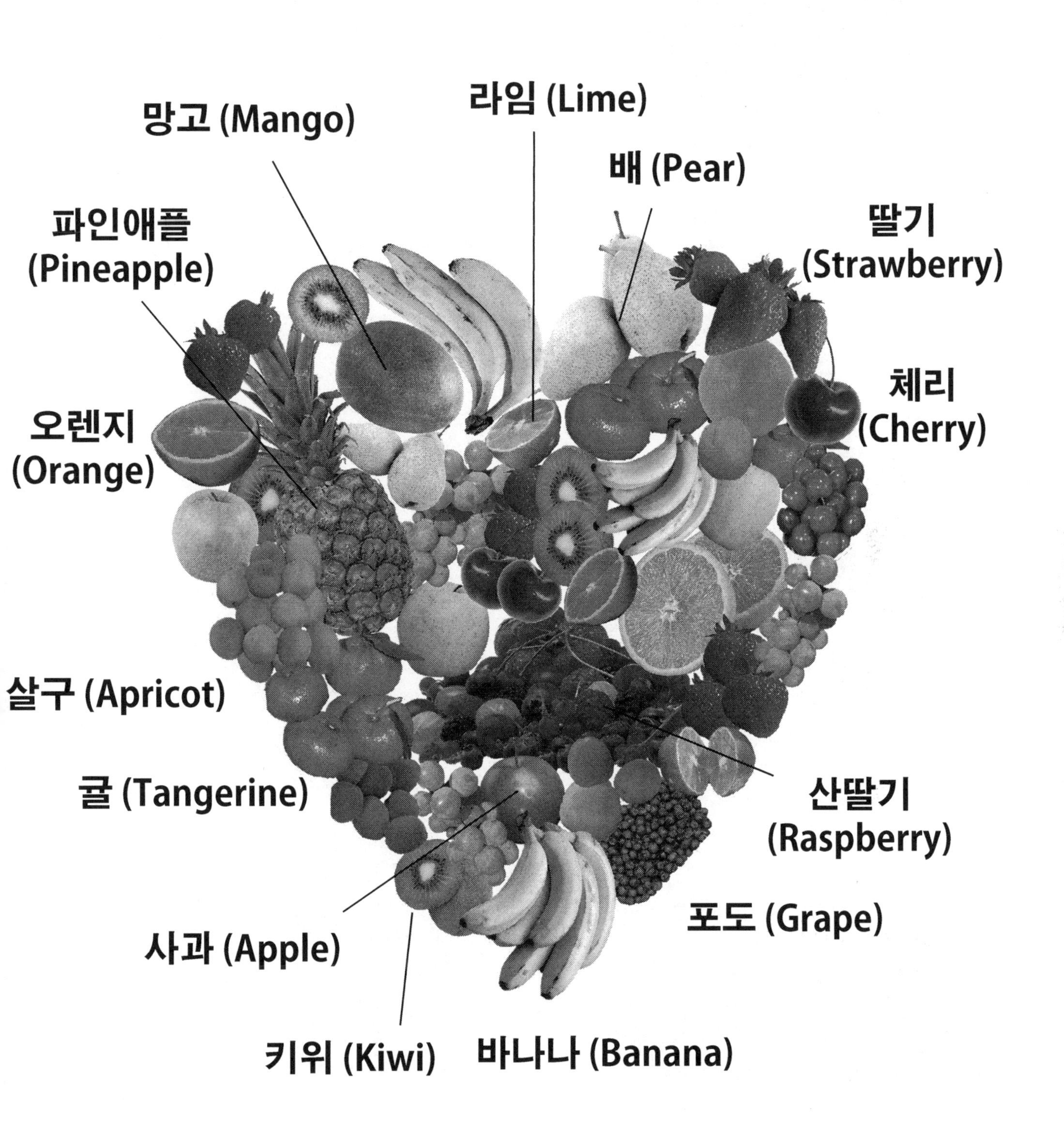

망고 (Mango)
라임 (Lime)
배 (Pear)
파인애플
(Pineapple)
딸기
(Strawberry)
체리
(Cherry)
오렌지
(Orange)
살구 (Apricot)
귤 (Tangerine)
산딸기
(Raspberry)
포도 (Grape)
사과 (Apple)
키위 (Kiwi)
바나나 (Banana)

수박 (Watermelon)

복숭아 (Peach)

석류 (Pomegranate)

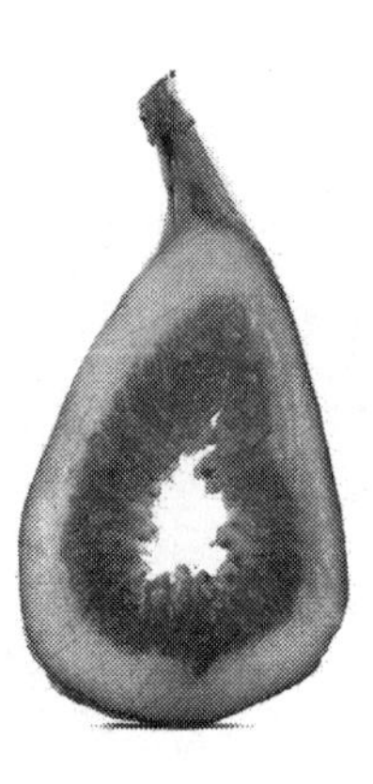

무화과 (Fig)

건포도 (Raisin)

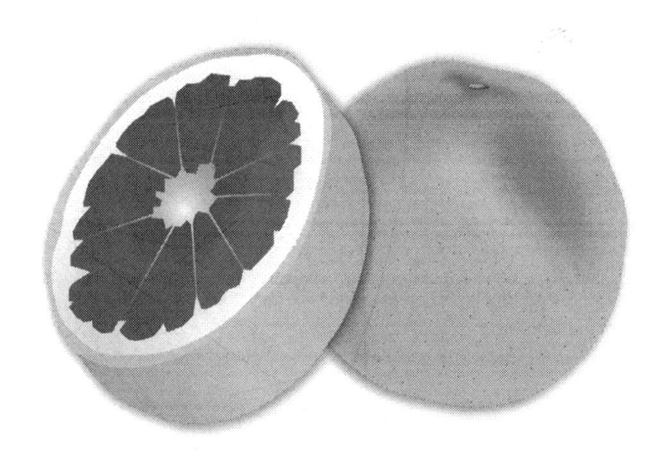

자몽 (Grapefruit)

호두 (Walnut)

땅콩 (Peanut)

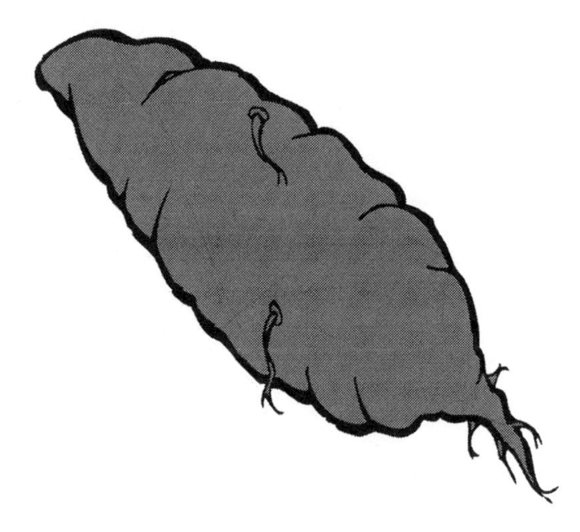

고구마 (Sweet Potato)

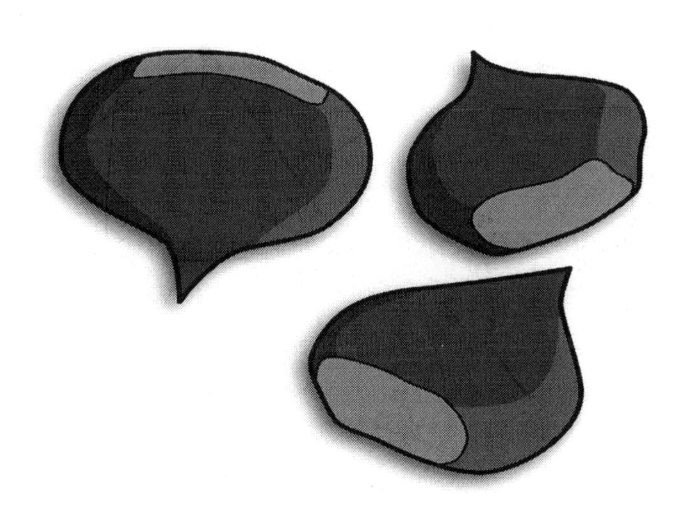

밤 (Chestnut)

양파 (Onion)

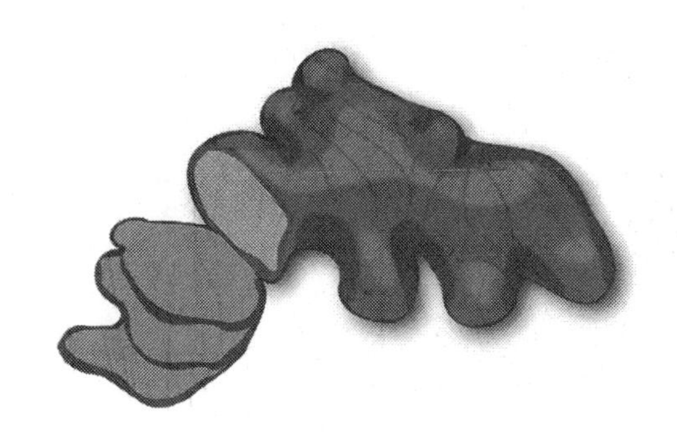

생강 (Ginger)

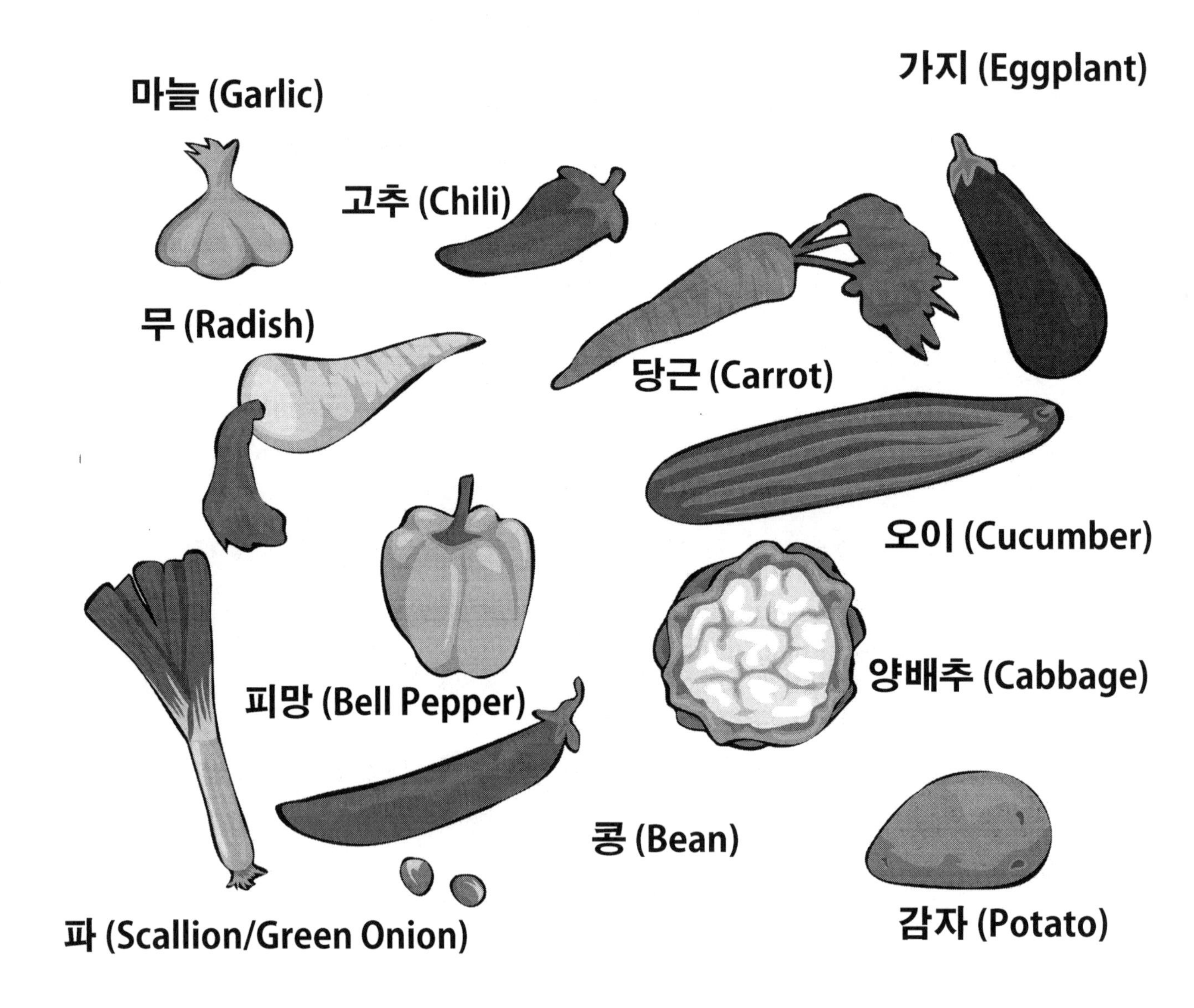
마늘 (Garlic)
가지 (Eggplant)
고추 (Chili)
무 (Radish)
당근 (Carrot)
오이 (Cucumber)
양배추 (Cabbage)
피망 (Bell Pepper)
콩 (Bean)
감자 (Potato)
파 (Scallion/Green Onion)

EXPRESSIONS(표현)

가시 없는 장미는 없다.
Every rose has its thorns.

불교에서 연꽃이 상징하는 바는 크다.
In Buddhism, lotus has lots of meanings.

벚꽃 구경하러 가자!
Let`s go cherry-blossom viewing!

원숭이는 바나나를 좋아해.
Monkeys like bananas.

갈증해소에는 수박이 최고다.
Watermelons are the best for quenching thirst.

복숭아 알러지가 있나요?
Are you allergic to peach?

고구마는 훌륭한 다이어트 식품이다.
Sweet potatoes are a great for weight loss.

양파는 나를 눈물나게 한다.
Onions make me cry.

호두는 까기가 정말 힘들다.
Walnuts are really difficult to crack open.

생강은 몸을 따뜻하게 한다.
Ginger warms up your body.

SCHOOL(학교)

교실 (Classroom)
선생님 (Teacher)
학생 (Student)
칠판 (Blackboard)
2+3=5
3+4=
책상 (Desk)

연필 (Pencil)

지우개 (Eraser)

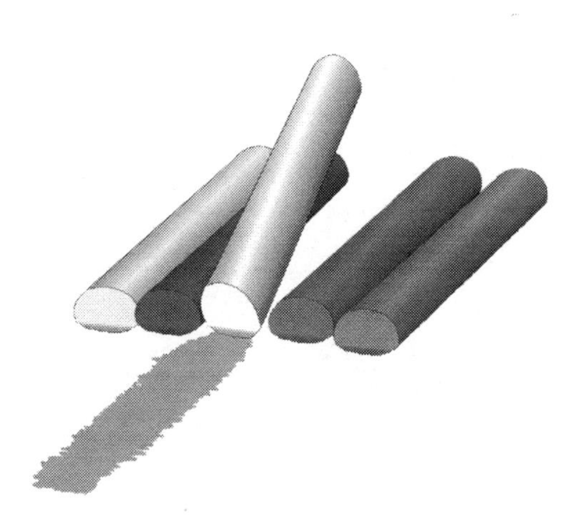

분필 (Chalk)

샤프 (Mechanical Pencil)

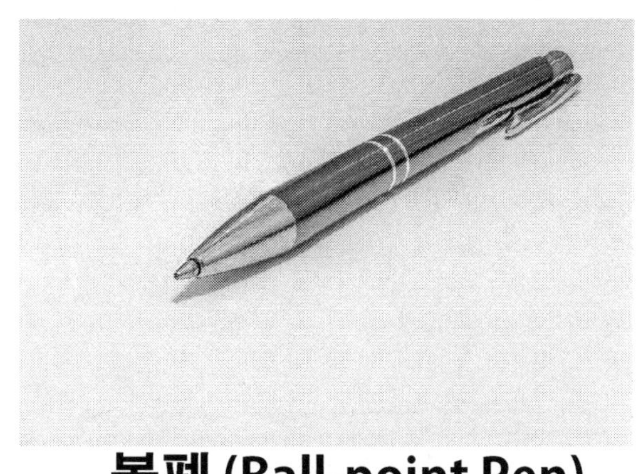

볼펜 (Ball-point Pen)

공책 (Notebook)

책 (Book)

책가방 (Backpack)

도시락 (Box Lunch)

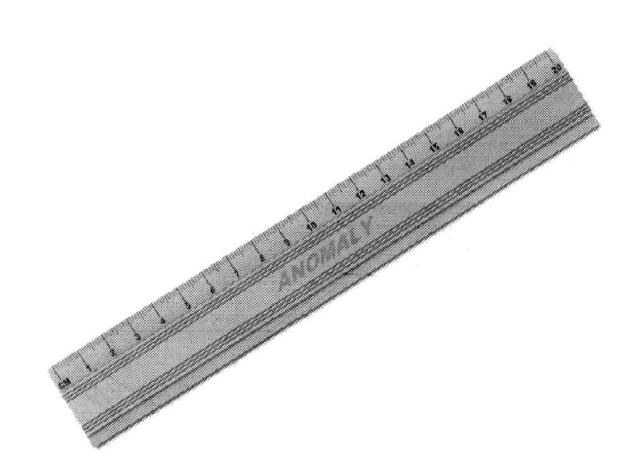

자 (Ruler)

체육관 (Gym)

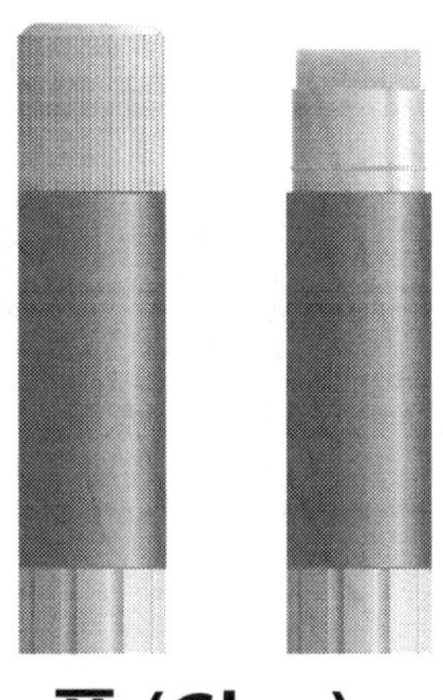

풀 (Glue)

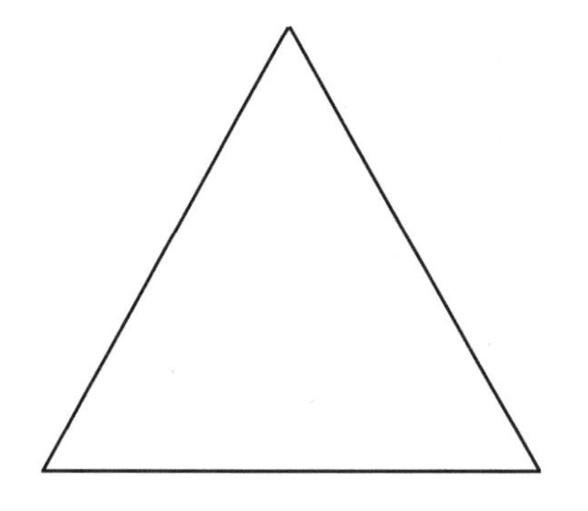

삼각형 (Triangle)

직사각형 (Rectangle)

정사각형 (Square)

오각형 (Pentagon)

육각형 (Hexagon)

원 (Circle)

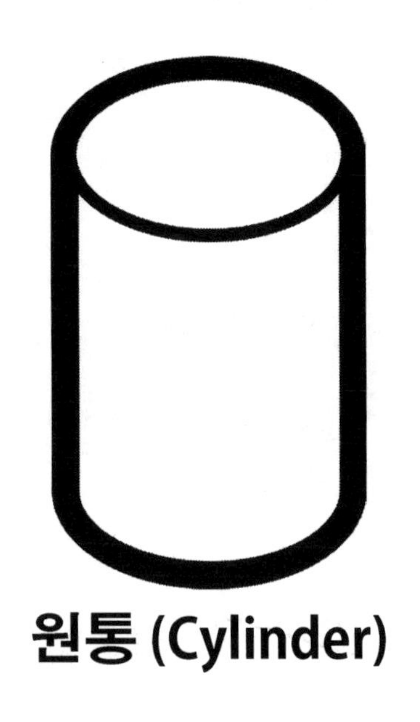

원통 (Cylinder)

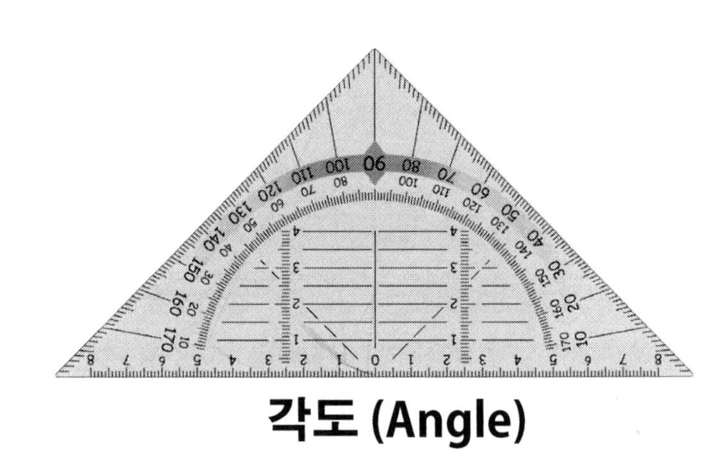

각도 (Angle)

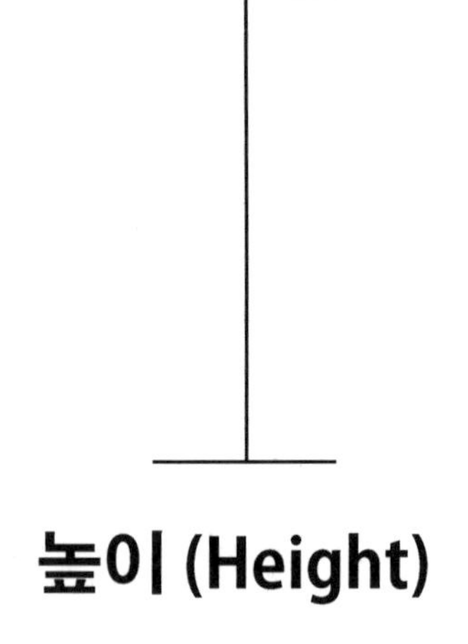

높이 (Height)

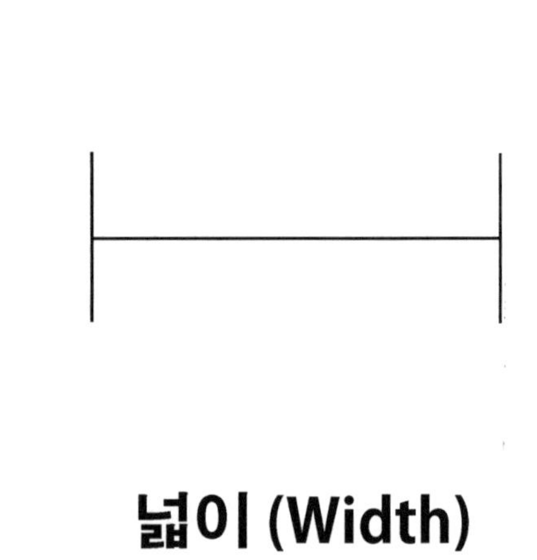

넓이 (Width)

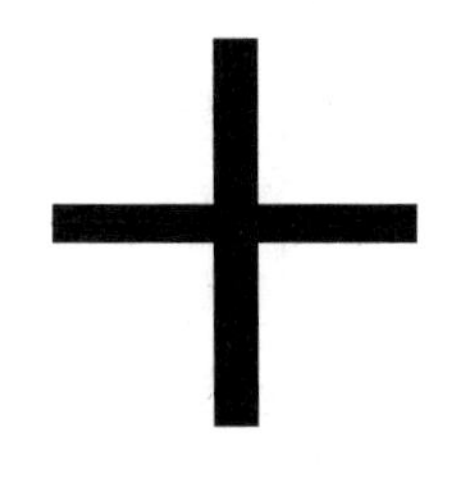

더하기 (Addition)

빼기 (Subtraction)

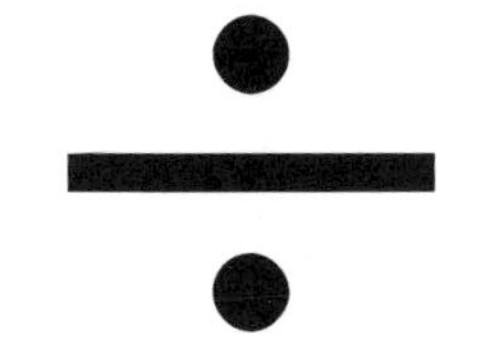

나누기 (Division)

곱하기 (Multiplication)

=

등호 (Equal Sign)

1/3

분수 (Fraction)

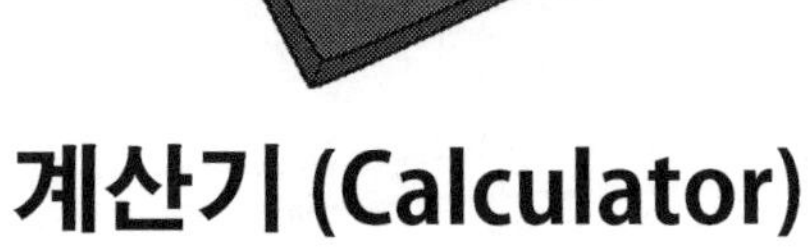

계산기 (Calculator)

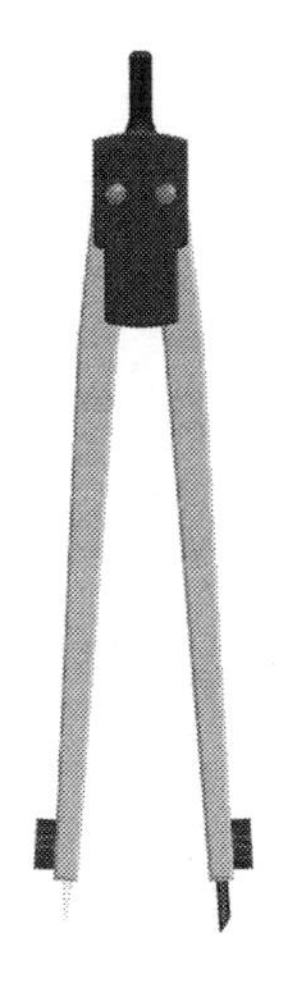

컴퍼스 (Compass/Divider)

EXPRESSIONS(표현)

연필을 깎아라 (command).
Sharpen your pencil.

지우개는 먹는것이 아니다.
Erasers are not something you eat.

공책에 적어라 (command)
Write it down in your notebook.

너 책가방이 좀 무겁지않니?
Isn`t your backpack a little heavy?

자가 부러졌다.
The ruler got broken.

책을 많이 읽어라 (command).
Read many books.

풀과 립스틱을 헷갈리지 말아라.
Do not confuse glue sticks with lipsticks.

원을 그려보자.
Let`s draw a circle.

삼각형은 세개의 선으로 이루어져있다.
A triangle is composed of three lines.

계산기를 사용해도 되나요?
Can I use a calculator?

SOLAR SYSTEM(태양계)

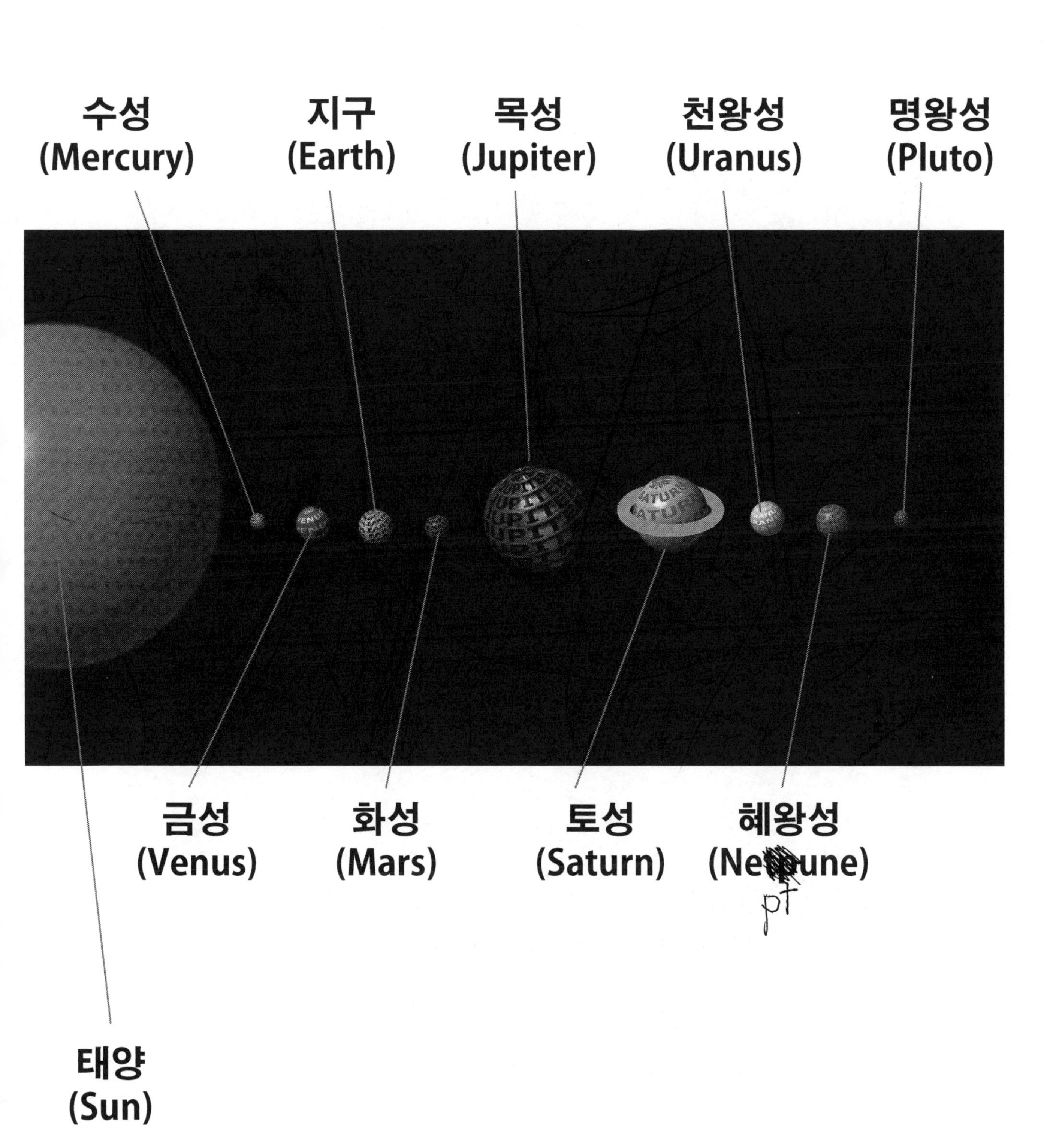

SOLAR SYSTEM(태양계)

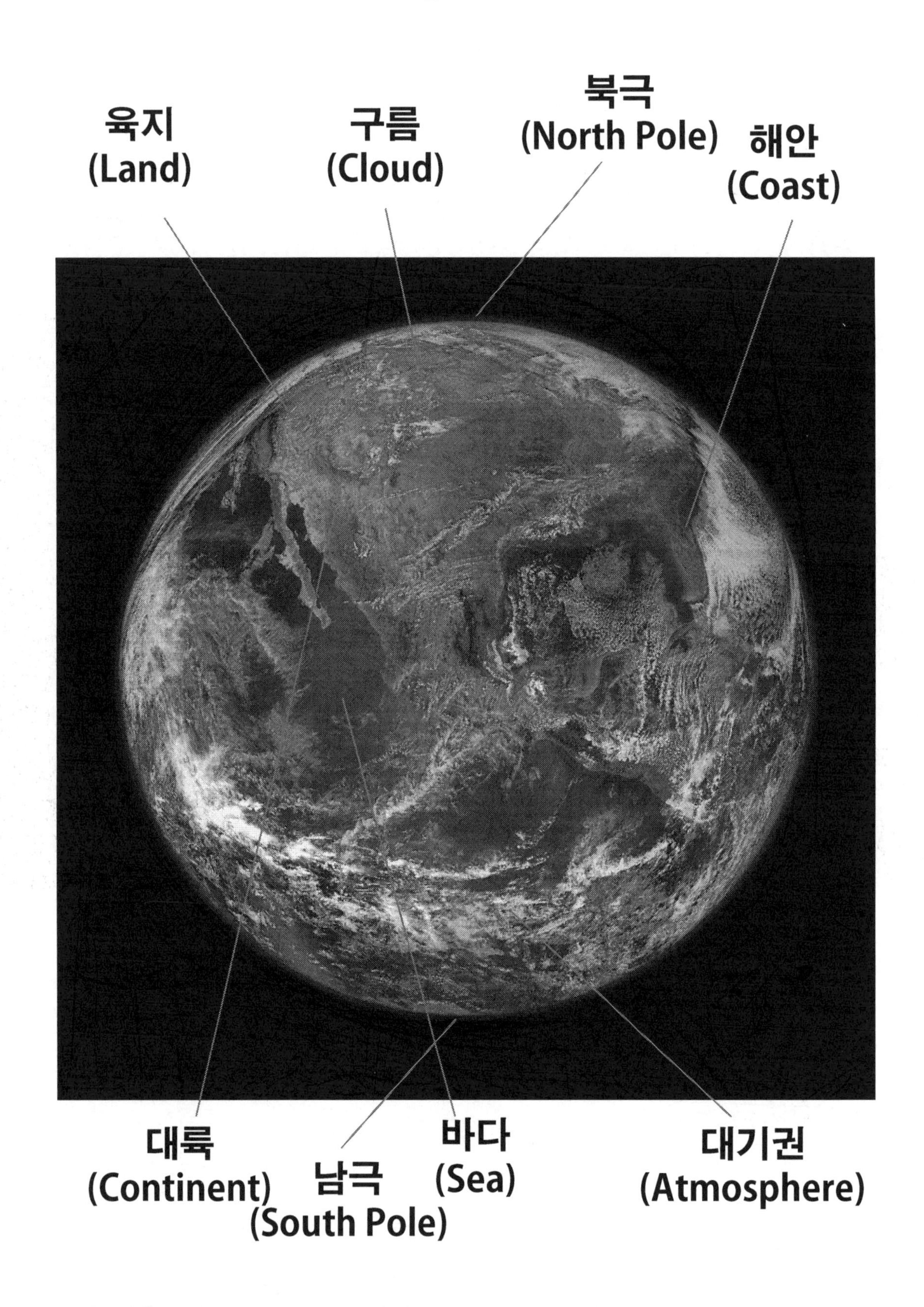

SOLAR SYSTEM (태양계)

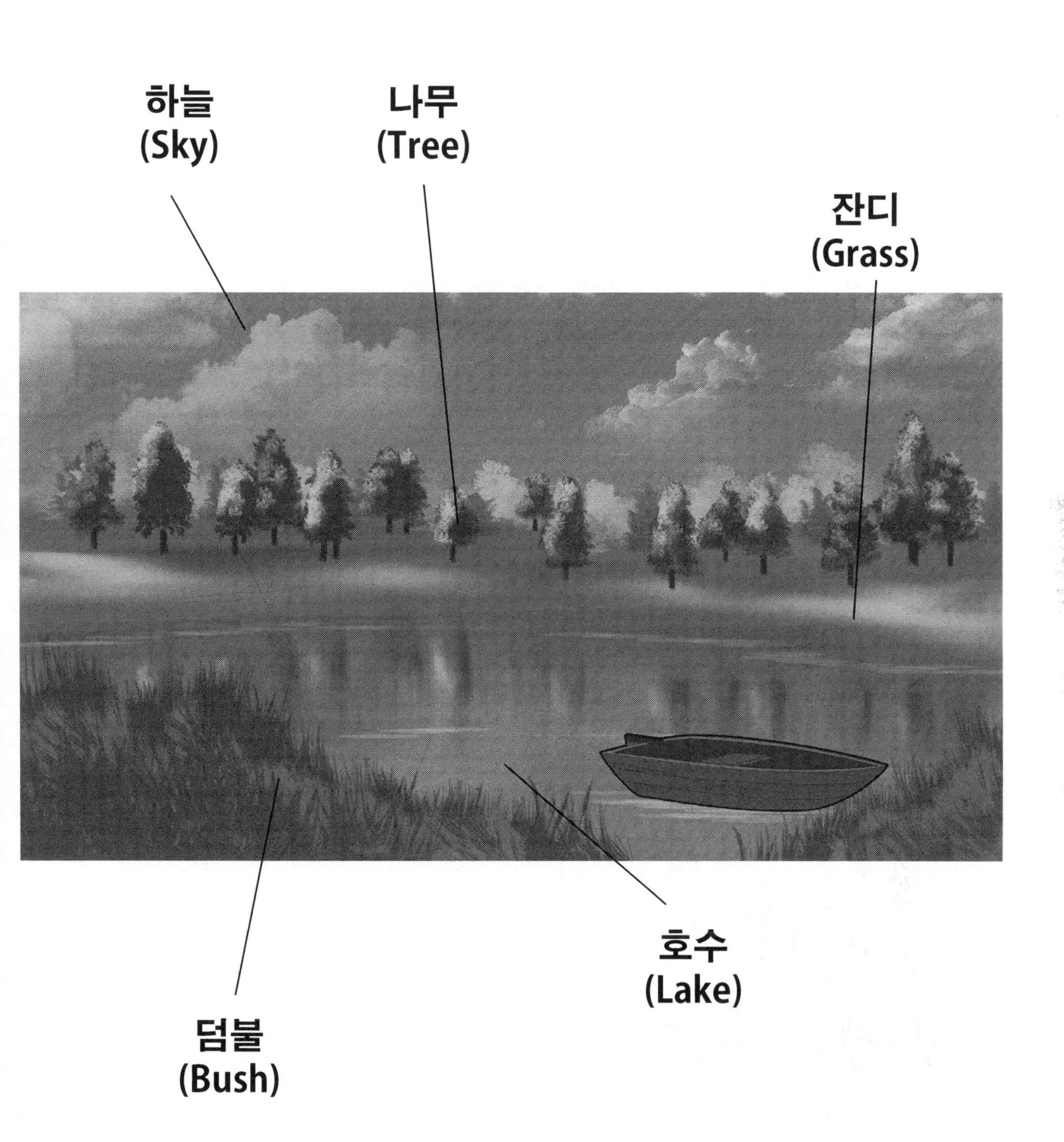

OUTDOORS(야외)

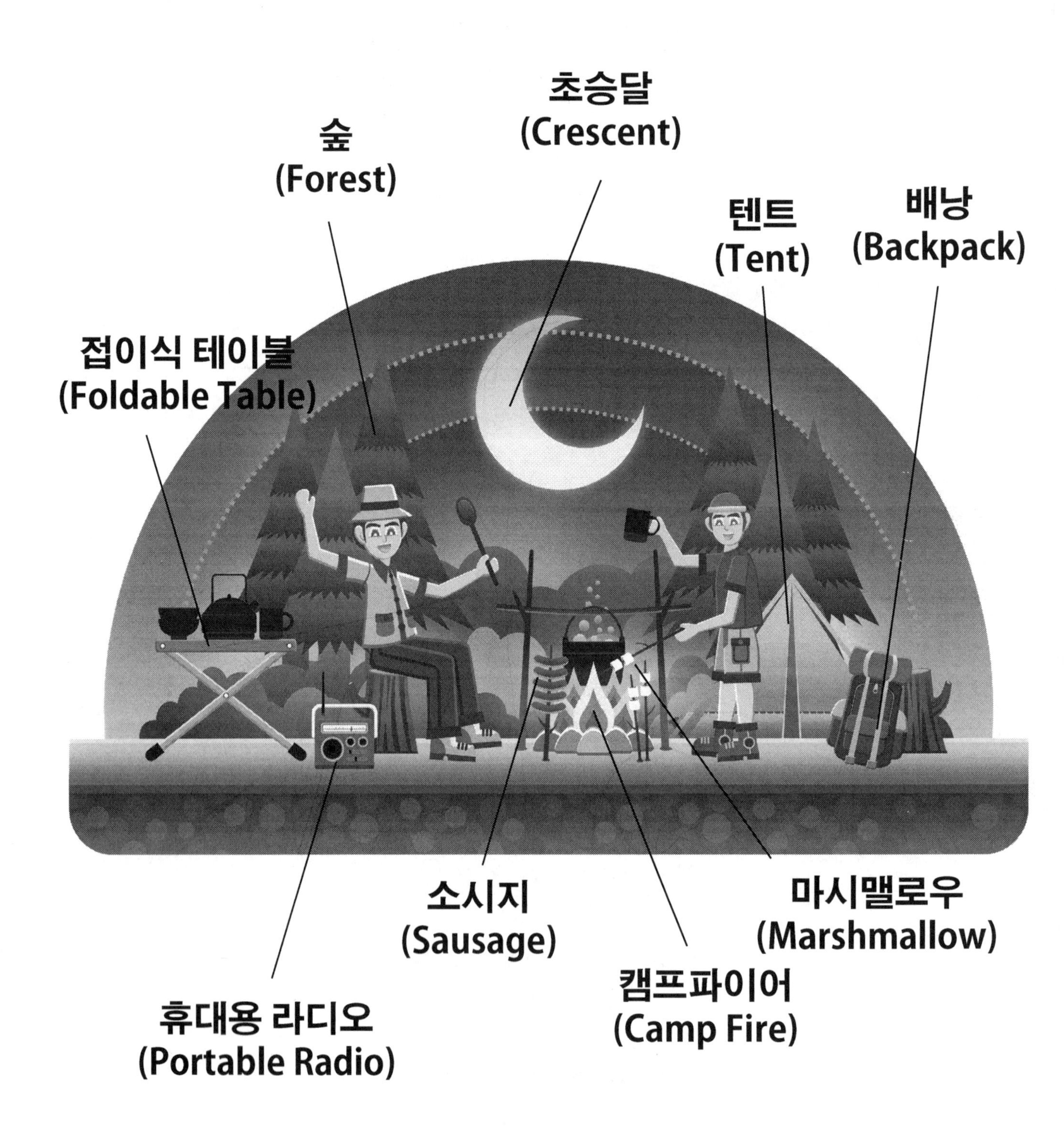
초승달
(Crescent)
숲
(Forest)
텐트
(Tent)
배낭
(Backpack)
접이식 테이블
(Foldable Table)
소시지
(Sausage)
마시맬로우
(Marshmallow)
캠프파이어
(Camp Fire)
휴대용 라디오
(Portable Radio)

EXPRESSIONS(표현)

지구는 태양 주위를 공전한다
The earth revolves around the sun.

육지를 향해 항해하다.
Sail towards the land.

북극에 도착하다.
Reach the North Pole.

해가 구름 뒤로 들어갔다.
The sun went behind a cloud.

대기권에 진입하다.
Enter the atmosphere.

아시아 대륙을 횡단하다.
Cross the Asian continent.

자동차가 해안을 따라 달렸다
The car drove along the coast.

What`s that in the sky?
하늘에 저게 뭐지?

A blade of grass.
풀잎 하나.

A tropical forest.
열대 숲

COLORS(색깔)

빨강 (Red)
주황 (Orange)
노랑 (Yellow)
초록 (Green)
파랑 (Blue)
남색 (Indigo)
보라 (Violet)

EXPRESSIONS(표현)

빨강은 사과의 색깔.
Red is the color of an apple.

주황은 오렌지의 색깔.
Orange is the color of an orange.

노랑은 바나나의 색깔.
Yellow is the color of a banana.

초록은 나무의 색깔.
Green is the color of trees.

파랑은 하늘의 색깔.
Blue is the color of the sky.

남색은 깊은 바다의 색깔.
Indigo is the color of the deep sea.

보라는 포도의 색깔.
Violet is the color of grapes.

APPAREL/ACCESSORIES (의류/악세사리)

바지 (Pants)

와이셔츠 (Dress Shirt)

티셔츠 (T-Shirt)

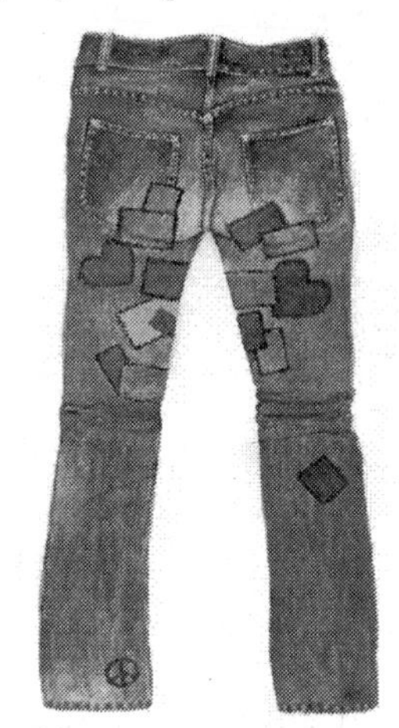

청바지 (Jean)

츄리닝 (Sweat Pants/Shirt)

양복/정장 (Suit)

드레스 (Dress)

자켓/잠바 (Jacket)

미니스커트 (Mini Skirt)

잠옷 (Sleepwear)

코트 (Coat)

반바지 (Short Pants)

수영복 (Swimsuit)

치마 (Skirt)

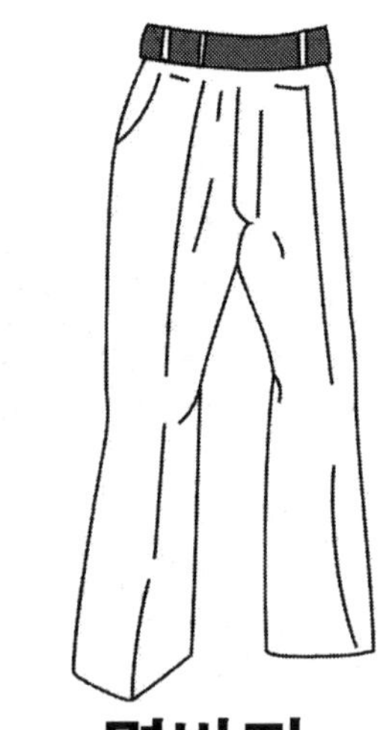

면바지
(Cotton Trousers)

폴로 셔츠 (Polo Shirt)

팬티 (Panties)

브라 (Bra)

모자 (Hat/Cap)

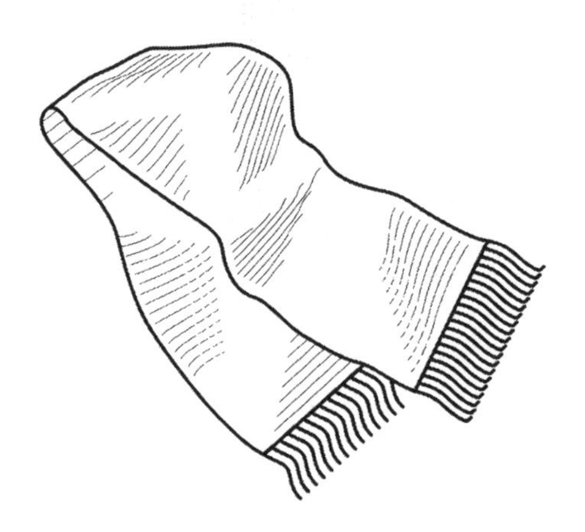

목도리/스카프
(Scarf/Muffler)

신발 (Shoes)

정장 구두 (Dress Shoes)

운동화 (Athletic Shoes)

양말 (Socks)

팔찌 (Bracelet)

목걸이 (Necklace)

귀걸이
(Earring)

반지 (Ring)

손목시계 (Watch)

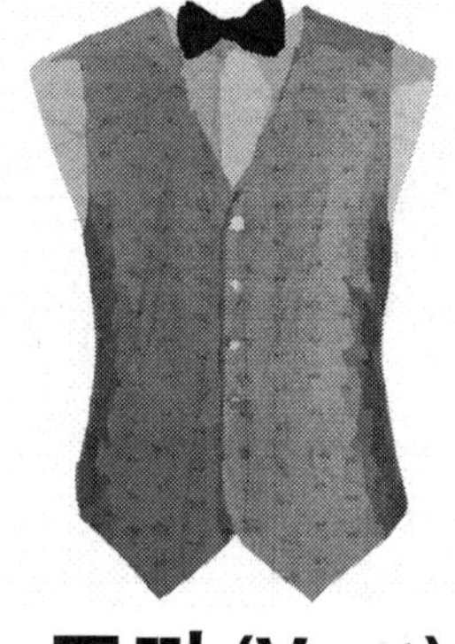

조끼 (Vest)

안경 (Glasses)

선글래스 (Sun Glasses)

슬리퍼 (Slippers)

쪼리/샌들 (Flip Flops)

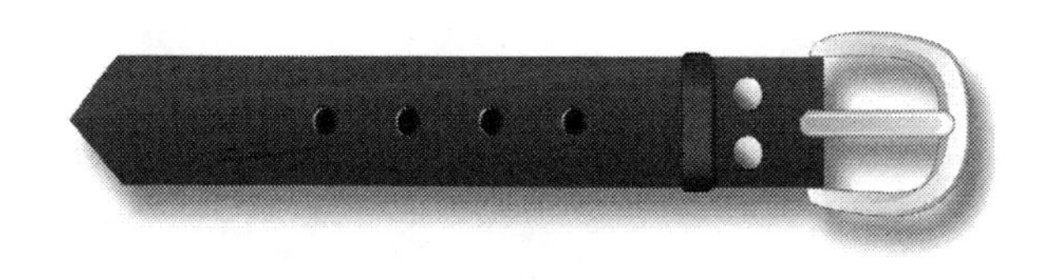

벨트 (Belt)

넥타이 (Tie)

EXPRESSIONS(표현)

너 바지가 너무 짧은거 아니니?
Aren`t your pants too short?

와이셔츠를 다려주세요.
Could you please iron my dress shirt?

츄리닝 입지 말고 정장 입으세요.
No sweatshirt. Wear a suit.

잠옷으로 갈아입다.
Change into sleepwear.

잠바 입는게 좋을 것 같다.
I think you`d better put on a jacket.

더운날에는 면바지가 좋다.
Cotton trousers are best for hot days.

저 사람 양말이 화려하네.
That guy`s socks are colorful.

내 시계가 멈췄다.
My watch stopped.

쪼리 신고 해변에 가자!
Let`s go to the beach wearing flip flops!

내 안경이 깨졌다.
My glasses are broken.

FEMALE PRODUCTS (여성용품)

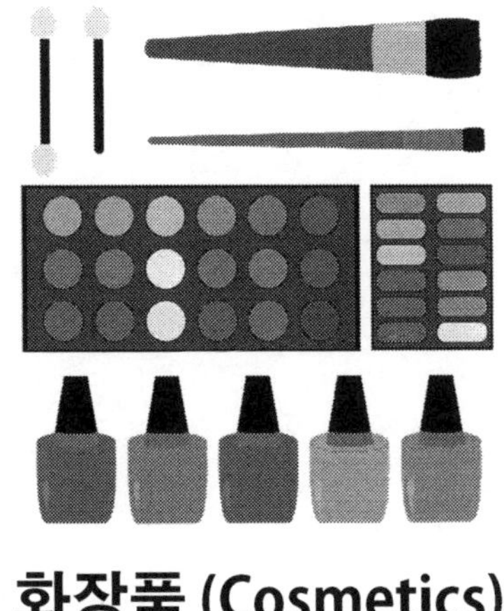

화장품 (Cosmetics)

머리띠 (Headband)

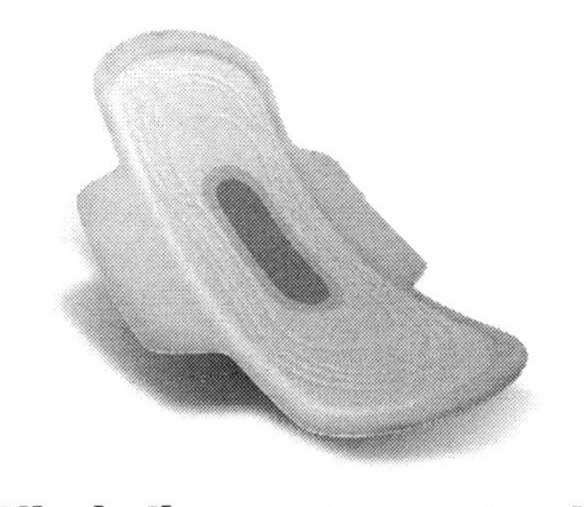

생리대 (Sanitary Pad)

클렌저/세안제
(Face Cleanser)

마스카라 (Mascara)

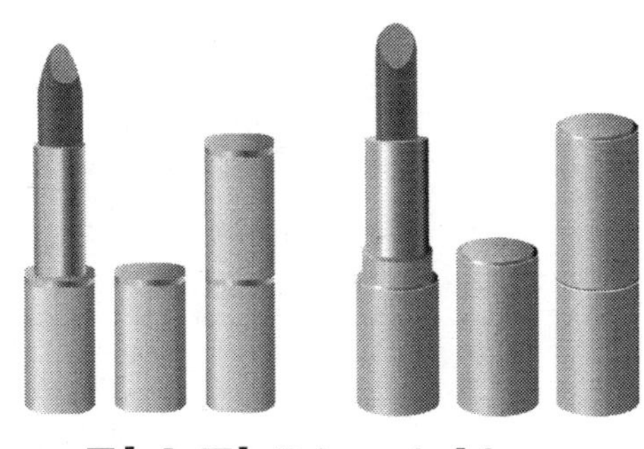

립스틱 (Lipstick)

향수 (Perfume)

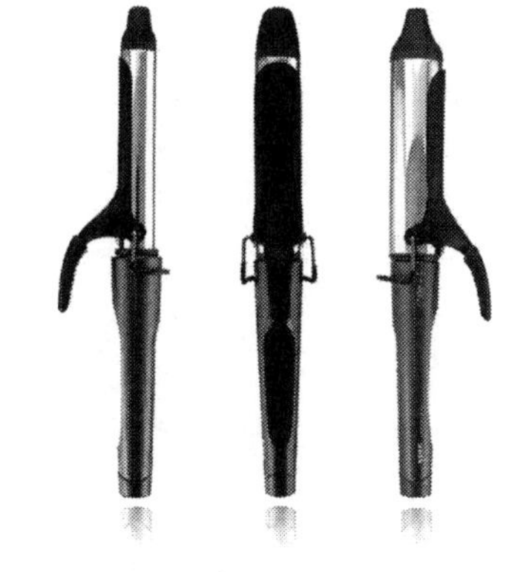

고데기 (Curling Iron)

빗 (Brush)

가발 (Wig)

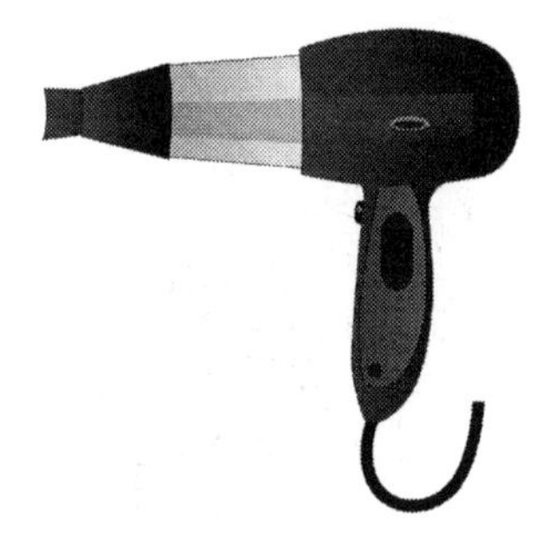

헤어드라이기 (Hair Dryer)

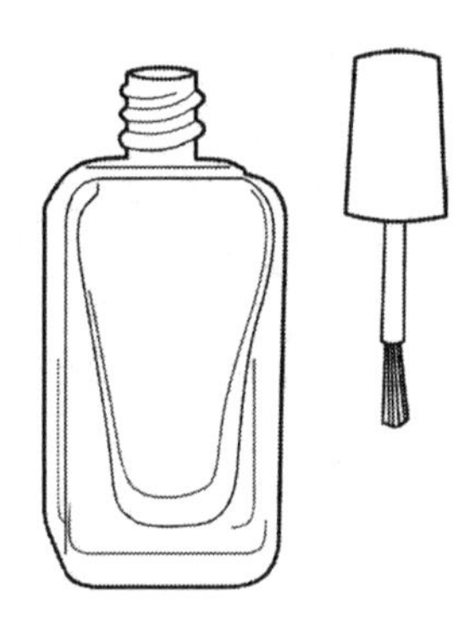

매니큐어 (Manicure)

MALE PRODUCTS (남성용품)

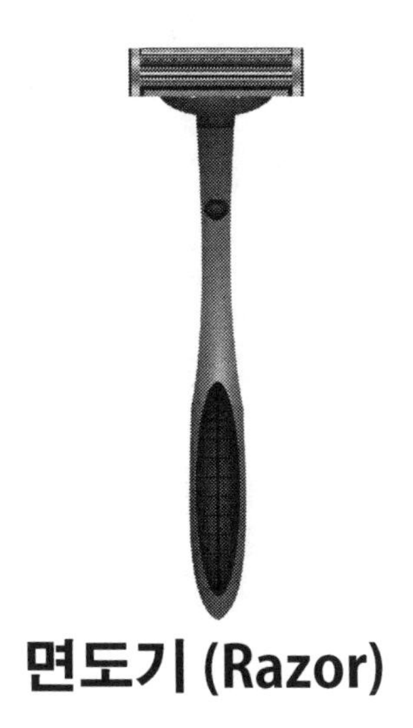

면도기 (Razor)

전기면도기 (Electric Shaver)

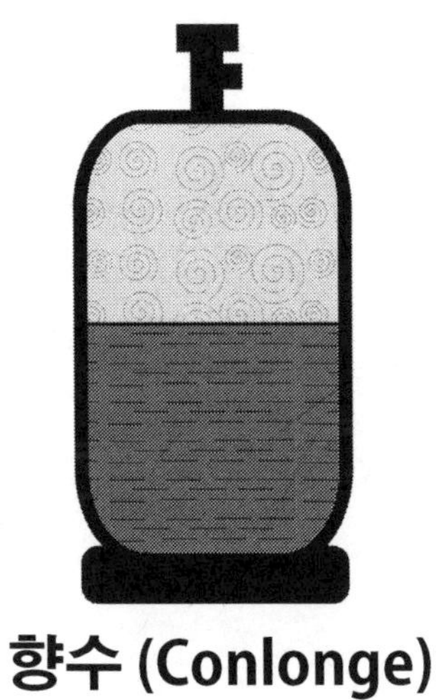

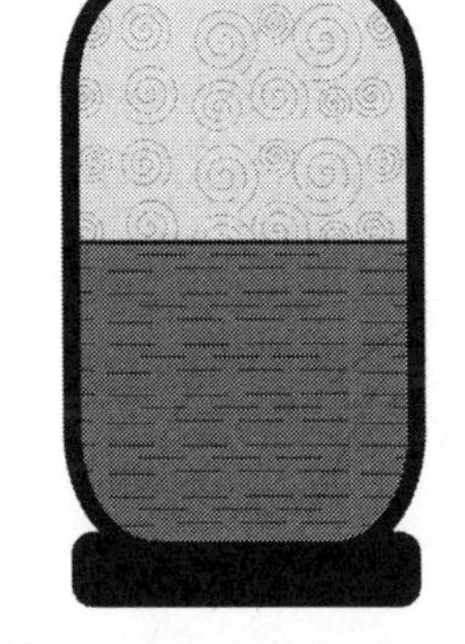

향수 (Conlonge)

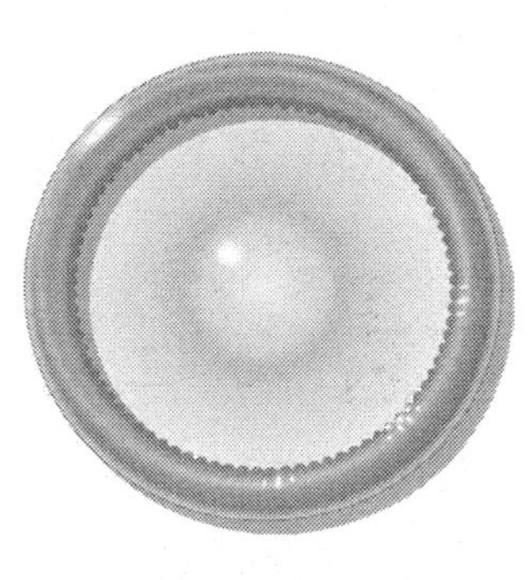

콘돔 (Condom)

서류가방 (Briefcase)

구두주걱 (Shoe Horn)

EXPRESSIONS(표현)

화장품에 돈을 너무 많이 쓰지 말거라 (command).
Don`t spend too much money on cosmetics.

머리띠를 하면 도움이 많이 된다.
Putting on a haeadband helps a lot.

생리대는 부끄러운 것이 아니다.
Sanitary pads are nothing to be ashamed of.

이 향수 냄새는 너무 진하다.
This perfume smells too strong.

고데기가 너무 뜨거우니 조심해!
The curling iron is too hot! Be careful!

전기면도기는 편리하다.
Electric shavers are convenient.

구두주걱 어디있지?
Where is the shoe horn?

서류가방 잊지 마세요!
Don`t forget the briefcase!

빗 여기 있어요.
Here`s a comb.

가발을 쓰고 있습니다.
I am wearing a wig.

RESTAURANT(레스토랑/식당)

포크 (Fork)

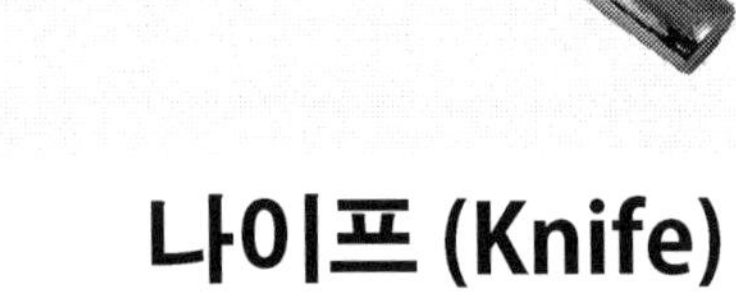

나이프 (Knife)

젓가락 (Chopsticks)

숫가락 (Spoon)

그릇 (Bowl)

밥그릇 (Rice Bowl)

접시 (Dish/Plate)

식탁보 (Tablecloth)

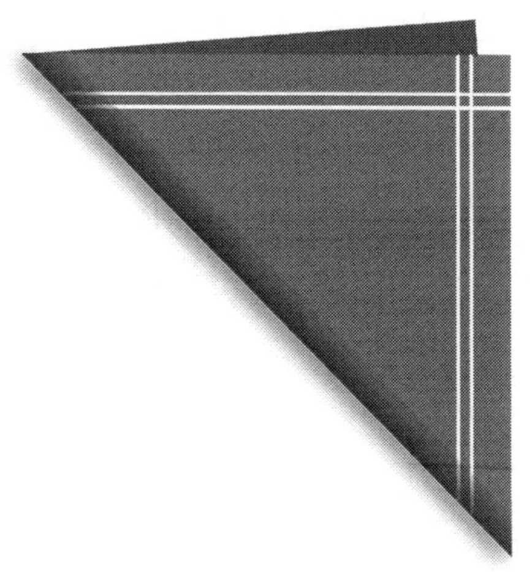

냅킨 (Napkin)

잔 (Glass)

소스 (Sauce)

양념 (Condiments)

계산서 (Bill)

턱받이 (Bib)

요리사/주방장 (Chef/Cook)

예약 (Reservation)

주문 (Order)

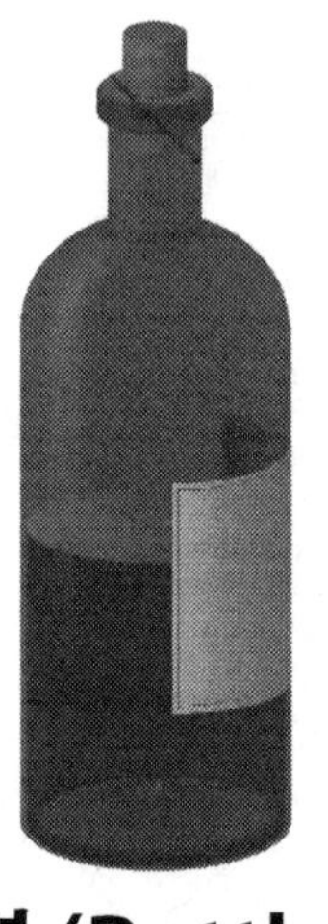

병 (Bottle)

EXPRESSIONS(표현)

아기가 턱받이에 침을 흘렸다.
The baby drooled onto the bib.

예약좀 해주세요!
Please make a reservation for me!

요리사가 새로운 디저트를 개발했다.
The chef invented a new dessert.

계산서 갖다주세요..
Please bring me the bill.

소주 한병!
A bottle of soju!

주문하시겠어요?
Would you like to order?

식탁보가 참 예쁘네요.
The tablecloth is so pretty.

젓가락질은 힘들어요,
Using chopsticks is difficult.

양념은 어디에 있나요?
Where are the condiments?

와인 한잔!
A glass of wine!

FOOD/BEVERAGE (음식/음료)

요리 (Cuisine)

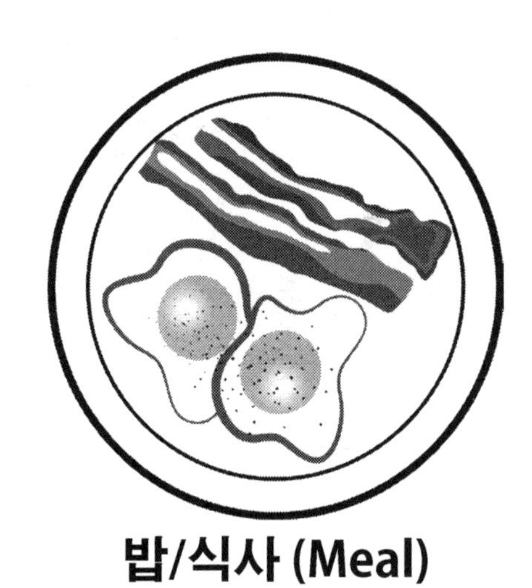

밥/식사 (Meal)

정식 (Prix Fixe)

간식 (Snack)

도시락 (Box Lunch)

통닭 (Whole Chicken)

계란/달걀 후라이 (Fried Egg)

김 (Seaweed)

국수 (Noodles)

밥 (Rice)

반찬 (Side Dishes)

생선구이 (Grilled Fish)

커피 (Coffee)

차 (Tea)

스포츠 음료 (Sports Drink)

우유 (Milk)

콜라 (Cola)

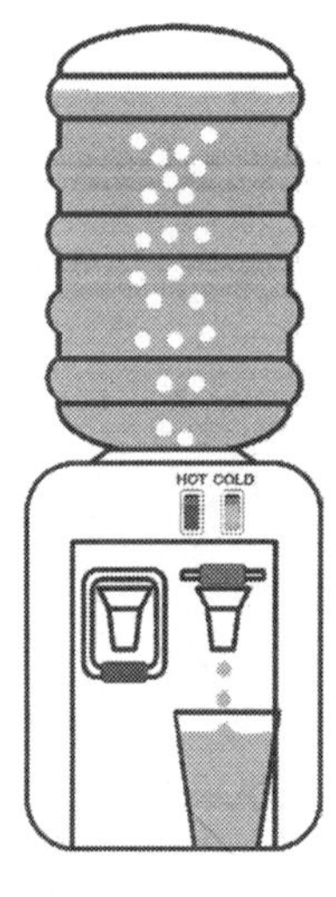

물 (Water)

얼음물 (Ice Water)

쥬스 (Juice)

탄산수 (Sparking Water)

맥주 (Beer)

술 (Alcoholic Drink)

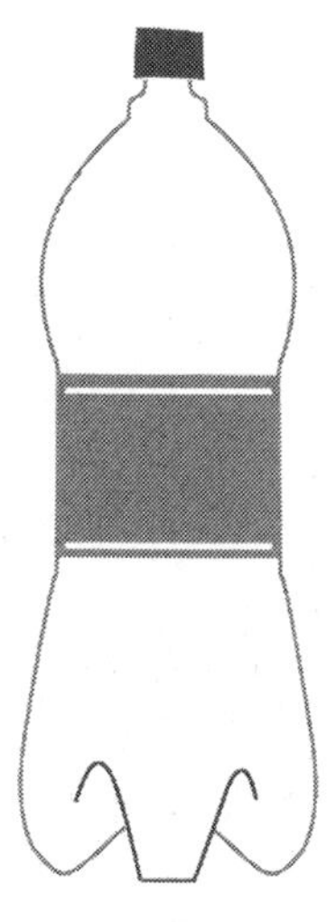

생수 (Bottled Water)

EXPRESSIONS(표현)

식사 하러 갑시다!
Let`s go for a meal!

간식으로 무엇을 먹을까?
What should I have for snack?

한식에는 반찬이 많이 나온다.
Korean cuisines are served with lots of side dishes.

달걀 후라이 두개.
Two fried eggs.

커피때문에 잠을 못잤다.
I could`t sleep because of coffee.

탄산수는 상쾌해.
Sparking water is so refreshing.

맥주 마시면 뚱뚱해져.
Drinking beer will make you fat.

쥬스가 신선하네!
The juice is fresh!

얼음물 아니면 차?
Ice water or tea?

스포츠 음료가 제일 효과적이다..
Sports drinks are most effeictve.

CALENDAR(달력)

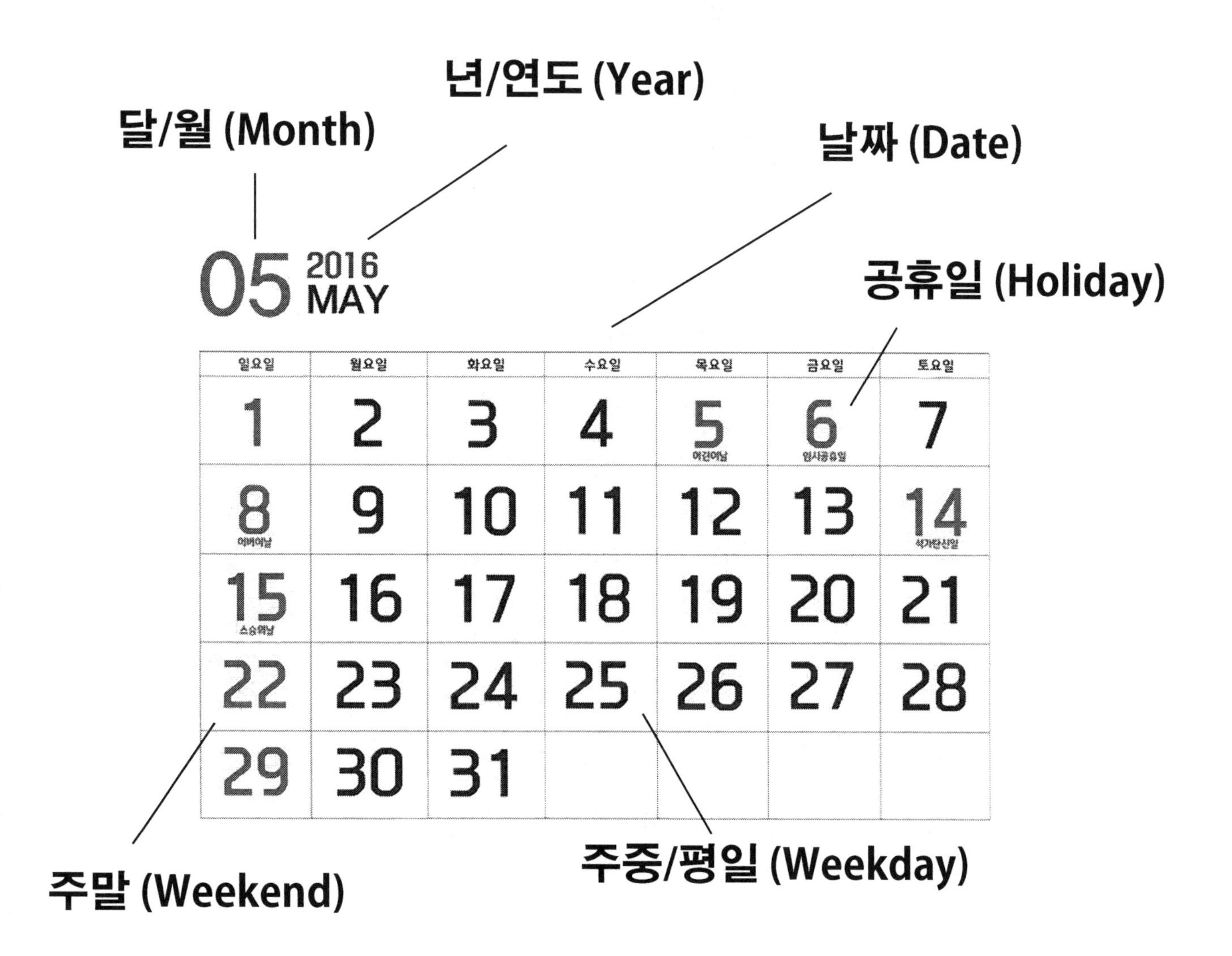

월요일 (Monday) 화요일 (Tuesday)

수요일 (Wednesday) 목요일 (Thursday)

금요일 (Friday) 토요일 (Saturday) 일요일 (Sunday)

EXPRESSIONS(표현)

2017년 5월 12일
May 12, 2017

오늘 공휴일이야?
Is today a holiday?

주말에 뭐해?
What are you doing on the weekend?

평일은 지루해.
Weekdays are boring.

날짜가 정확히 언제야?
What is the exact date?

월요일이 최악이다.
Mondays are the worst.

금요일이 제일 신난다.
Fridays are the most exciting.

일요일엔 좀 쉬자!
Let`s rest on Sunday!

이번 토요일에 바빠?
Are you busy this Saturday?

SEASONS/WEATHER(계절/날씨)

흐린 (Cloudy)

맑은/화창한 (Sunny)

천둥 번개
(Thunder and Lightning)

우박 (Hail)

눈 (Snow)

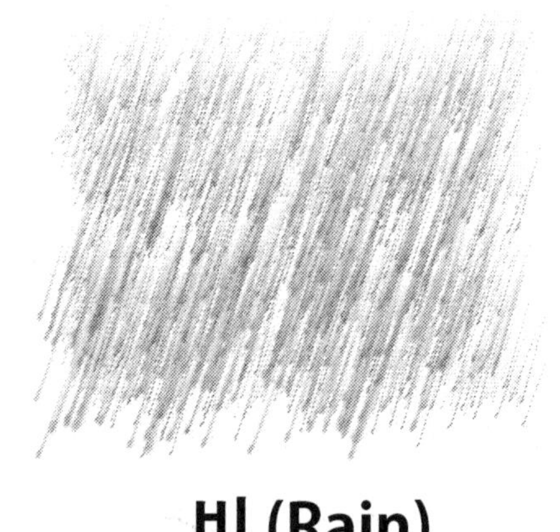

비 (Rain)

강풍 (Strong Wind)

미세먼지 (Fine Dust)

장마 (Summer Monsoon)

가뭄 (Drought)

홍수 (Flood)

폭설 (Heavy Snow)

지진 (Earthquake)

화산 폭발
(Volcano Eruption)

쓰나미 (Tsunami)

산사태 (Landslide)

눈사태 (Avalanche)

태풍 (Typhoon)

EXPRESSIONS(표현)

나는 여름에 태어났다.
I was born in the summer.

겨울에는 옷을 껴입어야지.
You need to bundle up in the winter.

봄이 느껴진다!
Spring is in the air!

미세먼지때문에 죽겠다!
Fine dust is killing me!

맑은 날에 우박?
Hail on a sunny day?

폭설이 오면 학교가 쉴까?
Would school close if we have a snow storm?

가뭄은 언제 끝날까?
When will the drought end?

지진인가?
Was that an earthquake?

쓰나미 경보!
Tsunami warning!

태풍이 온다!
Hurricane is coming!

PLACES(장소)

우체국 (Post Office)

경찰서 (Police Station)

도서관 (Library)

소방서 (Fire Station)

백화점 (Department Store)

공원 (Park)

노래방 (Karaoke)

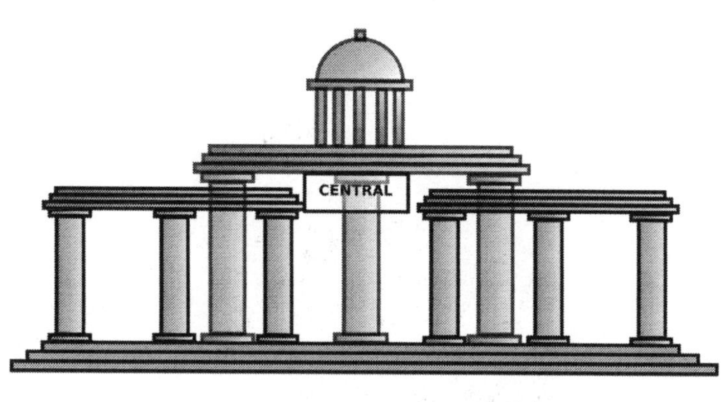

City Hall (시청)

병원 (Hospital)

Bank (은행)

영화관 (Movie Theater)

교회 (Church)

해변 (Beach)

버스 정거장 (Bus Stop)

동물원 (Zoo)

박물관 (Museum)

놀이터 (Playground)

놀이공원 (Amusement Park)

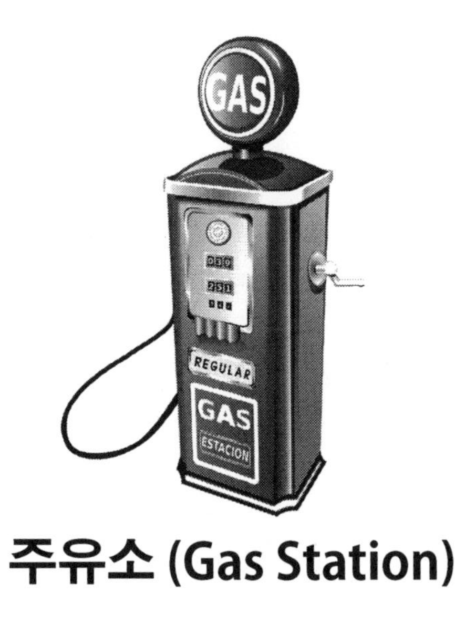

주유소 (Gas Station)

편의점 (Convenient Store)

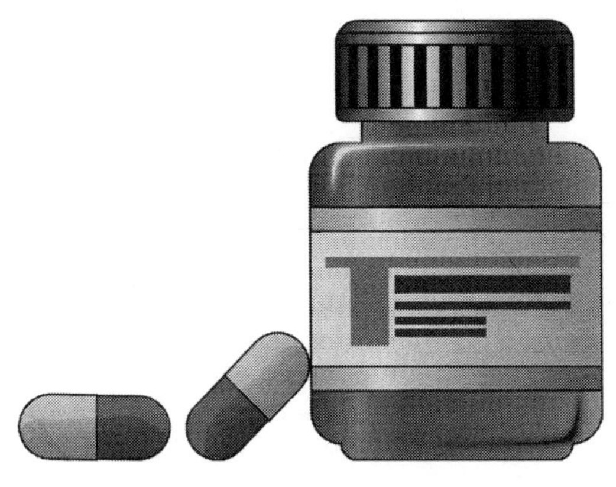

약국 (Drugstore)

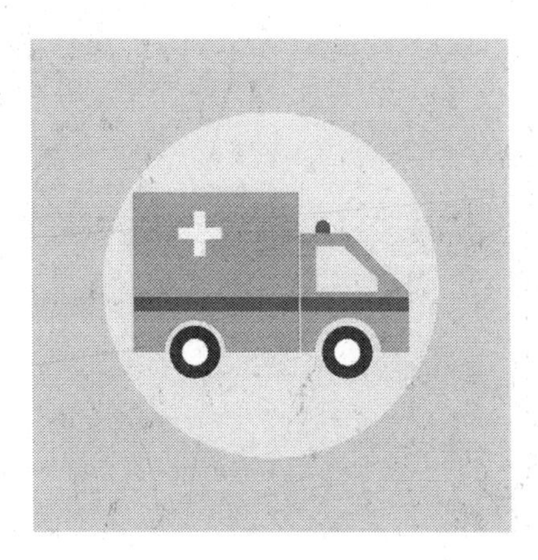

응급실 (Emergency Room)

찜질방 (Korean Spa/Sauna)

빵집 (Bakery)

EXPRESSIONS(표현)

경찰서로 갑시다!
Let`s go to the police station!

도서관에서 낮잠을 잤다.
I took a nap at the library.

다행히, 우리 집은 소방서에서 가까웠다.
Luckily, my house was close to the fire station.

우리는 노래방에서 즐거운 시간을 가졌다.
We had a fun time at the karaoke.

교회에가서 기도하자.
Let`s go to church and pray.

주유소에 잠깐 들리자.
Let`s stop by the gas station real quick.

응급실로 가주세요!
Take us to the emergency room!

동물원은 이상한 냄새가 난다.
The zoo has a funky smell.

놀이터는 아이들에게 재미있는 장소다.
Playgrounds are a fun place for kids.

편의점이 저기 있다!
There is a convenient store!

THINGS(물건)

우표 (Postage Stamp)

봉투 (Envelope)

수갑 (Handcuffs)

권총 (Pistol)

금고 (Safe/Vault)

사서 (Librarian)

소화기 (Fire Extinguisher)

소방차 (Fire Truck)

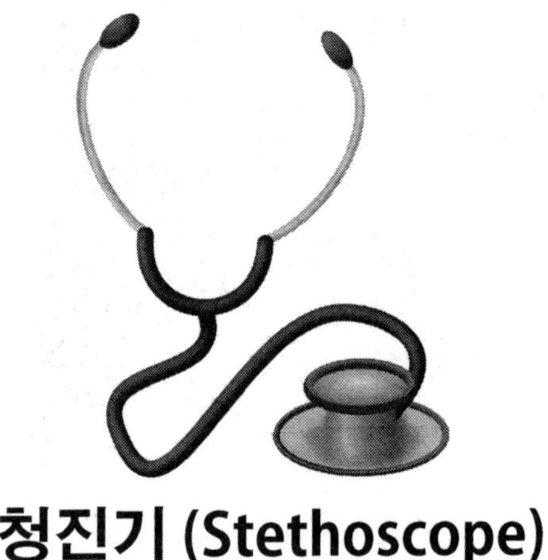

청진기 (Stethoscope)

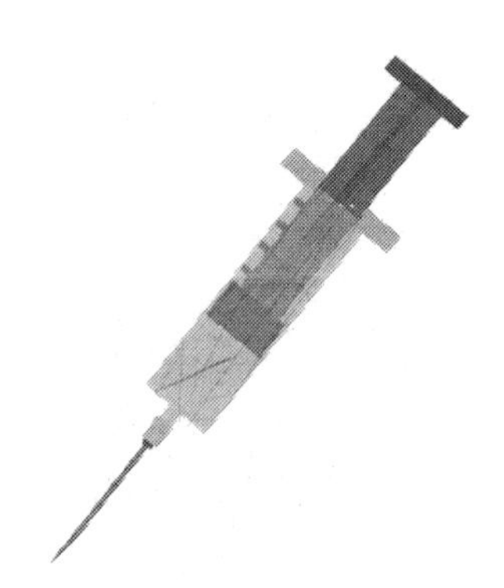

주사기 (Syringe)

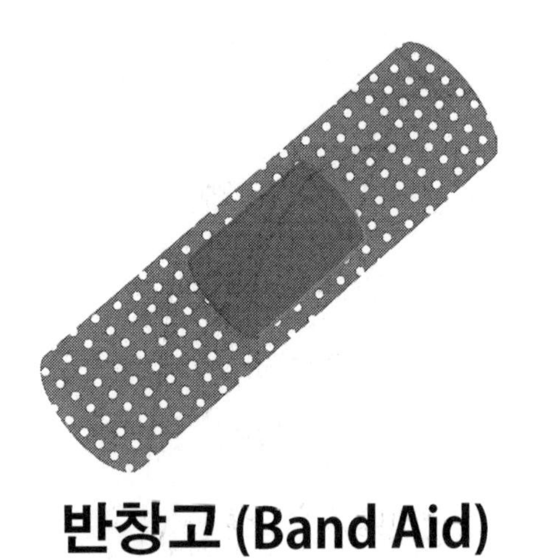

반창고 (Band Aid)

환자 (Patient)

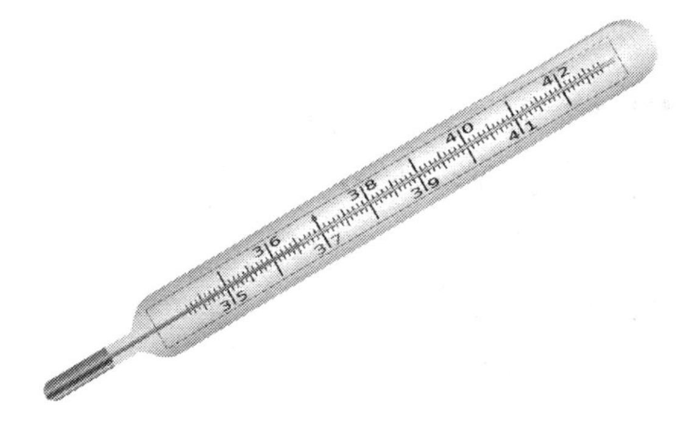

체온계 (Thermometer)

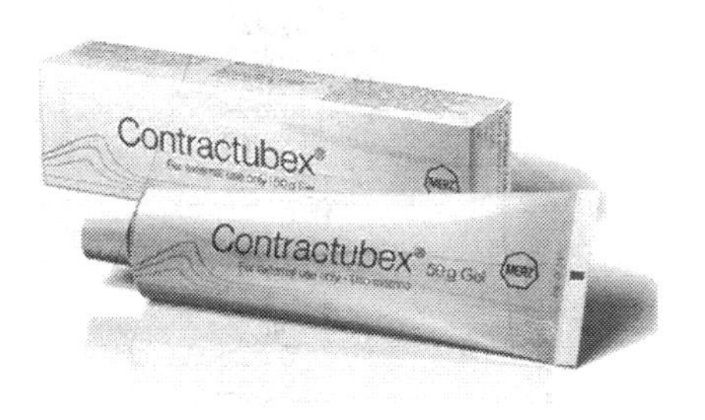

연고 (Ointment)

신부님 (Father)

수녀님 (Nun)

성체 (Communion)

십자가 (Cross)

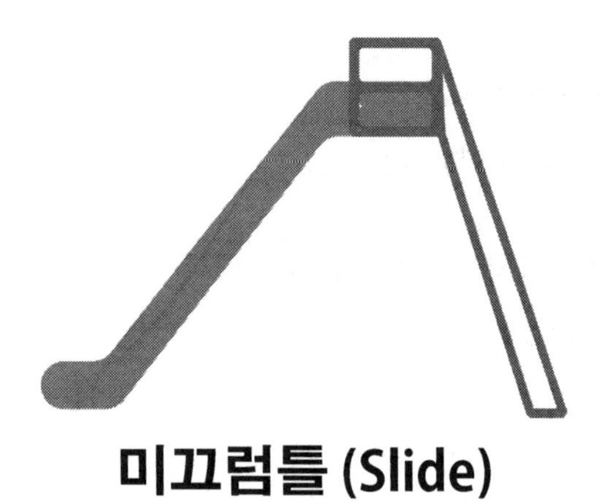

미끄럼틀 (Slide)

그네 (Swing)

은행원 (Banker)

지폐 (Paper Money)

동전 (Coin)

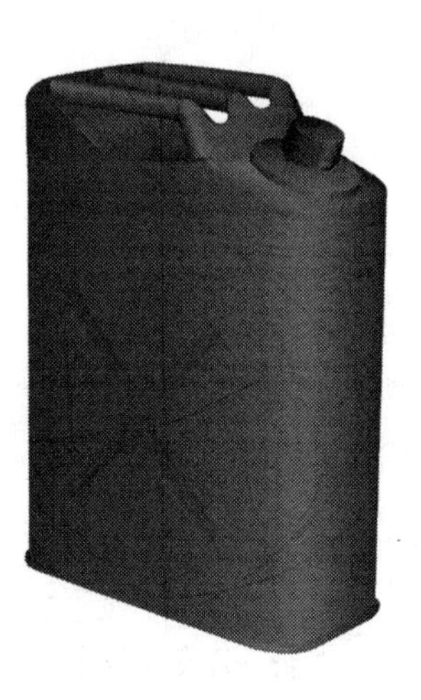

휘발유 (Gasoline)

EXPRESSIONS(표현)

봉투에 우표를 붙이세요.
Put a postage stamp on an envelope.

경찰관은 권총을 가져오는 것을 깜빡했다.
The policeman forgot to bring his pistol.

금고안에는 아무것도 없었다.
There was nothing in the safe.

사서는 지금 매우 바쁘다.
The librarian is very busy at the moment.

천주교 신부님
A Catholic father

살균 연고
Antiseptic ointment

제니는 수녀님이 되었다.
Jenny became a nun.

반창고 필요하세요?
Do you need a band-aid?

환자가 잠들었다.
The patient fell asleep.

의사가 그를 청진기로 진찰했다.
The doctor examined him with a stethoscope.